Summer Reading Program Fun

10 Thrilling, Inspiring, Wacky Board Games for Kids

Wayne L. Johnson
Yvette C. Johnson

AMERICAN LIBRARY ASSOCIATION
Chicago and London
1999

Project editor: Louise D. Howe

Cover and text design: Lucy Lesiak Design

Composition by the dotted i in Garamond and Cooper Black using QuarkXPress 3.32

Printed on 50-pound offset opaque, a pH-neutral stock, and bound in 10-point coated cover stock by McNaughton & Gunn

The paper used in this publication meets the minimum requirements of American National Standard for Information Sciences—Permanence of Paper for Printed Library Materials, ANSI Z39.48-1992. ∞

Library of Congress Cataloging-in-Publication Data

Johnson, Wayne L., 1942–
    Summer reading program fun : 10 thrilling, inspiring, wacky board games for kids /
  by Wayne L. Johnson and Yvette C. Johnson.
        p.   cm.
    ISBN 0-8389-0755-5
    1. Children's libraries—Activity programs. 2. Reading promotion. 3. Children—Books
  and reading. 4. Board games. I. Johnson, Yvette C. II. Title.
  Z718.1.J63 1999
  027.62′5—dc21   98-45378

Printed in the United States of America.

03 02 01 00 99   5 4 3 2 1

For our daughter, Victoria

Contents

Preface

Planning creative summer reading programs is a challenge. This book helps you with materials to create whimsical board games aimed at elementary school students, from kindergarten through grade five. The programs originate from the Glenview (Illinois) Public Library, where successful summer reading programs are a tradition. In a community of thirty-eight thousand, over two thousand youngsters participate in one of three available summer reading programs. Many visit the library daily. The three age-appropriate summer programs are structured quite differently. This book focuses on our K–5 program. The summer's program revolves around a single game. If you use them all, you have ten years of programming!

The program comprises three critical components. The first is listening to book reports. Each child gives a brief oral summary of a book before playing the game. As time-consuming as this can be, these brief reports are crucial to the success of the entire program. Staff and children gradually get to know each other by name. The familiarity strengthens a child's confidence and encourages library use the rest of the year. Furthermore, parents like to see their children practice speaking skills with adults. Often, when their children are reporting on a book, parents will stand unobtrusively just within earshot and listen. Usually they are delighted.

The second component is the game itself. After the oral book report, the child takes a turn at playing the board game. The games are especially exciting for the elementary school age group. They feature themes of high adventure, fantasy, or silliness. Creating and conducting the games is the stuff of this book.

The third component to this program is the giving of prizes. Youngsters love to earn prizes; and for those who struggle with reading skills, it can be just the motivation needed. Even for those with an intrinsic love of reading, a little prize can make the difference between whether one picks up a book or watches TV for an extra half hour. Our prizes are not fancy or expensive. Typical examples are erasers, keychains, bookmarks, Bentcils (pencils bent into cute shapes) and coupons redeemable at local businesses.

Children win some prizes by chance, others are earned. A youngster may win by chance by landing on a prize square on the board game. Other prizes are earned by reading a certain number of books. In twenty years at the library we have never once had a parent say "Stop giving prizes." Instead over the years hundreds and hundreds of parents have thanked us for giving their child an incentive to read over the summer. They see us as their ally, helping to make their job of motivating and educating a little easier.

Some children's librarians disagree with this approach. They seem to feel that prizes sully the "pure" act of reading, that children should love reading for its own sake. Certainly, we are all for a child developing an intrinsic love of reading, but we are also realistic.

Competition for a child's leisure time has never been keener than it is today. We need to keep this reality in the forefront of our program planning. Likely as not, the child at leisure is staring at a screen connected to an electronic device. The visuals are mesmerizing; the sound is fantastic. Our challenge is to keep the book competitive—especially over summer vacation.

One example of the power of a small prize is our specially made ribbon for reading at least five Newbery Award or Newbery honor books. Last year one of our fifth graders actually plowed through *The Story of Mankind* by Hendrick Van Loon in order to earn that ribbon!

To truly encourage reading, the game itself needs to grab the child's imagination. Nothing is more deadly than a boring game, especially one whose plot is literally tied into books and reading. Would a character named "Billy Book" or "Mary Mystery" whose quest is to reach "Library Land" inspire you to participate? Of course not. Happily, the games included here are guaranteed to entertain and motivate.

Our summer reading programs keep the computers in the Circulation Department on the brink of overheating, keep the parking lot crowded, attract curious onlookers from other departments, and generally notify the community at large that Something Is Going On at the Library.

We hope this book will help you achieve similar results and have a lot of fun while doing it. Keep in mind that the games in this book can be tailored to fit your particular facility or situation. Even if your library is small, you can use these games to build excitement into your summer reading program. So . . . let the games begin!

Graphics files for the games in this book
may be downloaded
from the ALA Editions Web site at

http://www.ala.org/editions/SRPFun

Acknowledgments

The summer reading program at the Glenview Public Library is a longstanding tradition which succeeds thanks to the cooperation and support of many people.

Over many years the Library Board of Trustees and administration have recognized the importance of this service for the community and have funded it with personnel and materials. The staff of Youth Services, past and present, have provided creative and lively input during the development of the programs. The inspired artwork of graphic artist Linda Hakey has contributed enormously to the success of the annual games at Glenview.

A final debt must be acknowledged to IREAD—Illinois Reading Enrichment and Development. A number of our games were modified to complement themes of their annual statewide summer reading programs, and many of our giveaway prizes were purchased from IREAD. For more information on this program, write to Illinois Library Association, 33 W. Grand Avenue, Suite 301, Chicago, IL 60610.

PART 1

Planning the Games

CHAPTER 1

Elements of the Games

Our summer reading program is centered around a board game that is set up in the children's area of the library. Playing pieces are advanced a certain number of squares on the board according to the drawing of a random number. The pieces on the board represent three teams, each of which is competing for the highest number of points. Points are scored as each piece reaches the end of the game path and accomplishes whatever goal the game involves. Once a piece has reached the last square, it is returned to the starting square to begin again.

A record of each team's score is kept on a scorecard mounted on the wall near the game board. Since only the team's score is recorded, children can enjoy playing the game whether they visit the library once or many times over the course of the summer.

THE GAME AREA The setup for the game consists of the following components, each of which will be described in greater detail in chapter 2:

The game board. This is the actual playing field for the game. We create ours on a large bulletin board, but most games in this book would work just as well on a tabletop. The board is decorated according to the theme for each year's game. A three- or four-inch wide game path, divided into squares, runs around the board.

The character/playing pieces. Three playing pieces representing the characters in the game are moved along the game path by advancing the number of squares indicated by a random number generator.

Random number generator. A fancy name for a simple spinner, die or pair of dice, or any other gadget that can produce a random number.

Scorecards and tokens. There is a scorecard for each character. These should be hung on a wall near the game board. Score tokens, representing a successful trip around the board by a character, are attached to the scorecards as they are earned.

Side tables. These are small tables set up near the game board. They are decorated in keeping with the game's theme, and usually contain some mechanism for helping a player select a prize. One of the tables' functions is to move players who have finished their turn and are entitled to prizes away from the game board so other players can take their turn. If long lines are not a problem at your library, you may choose to forgo the tables altogether.

Book form. A card or sheet of paper, one for each child, bearing the child's name and the names of all books the child has reported on. The book form is updated each time the child plays the game.

PLAYING THE GAME

Here is a brief walkthrough of the game as a typical player might experience it:

When a student comes into the library and says "I want to join the program," we ask if she has read a book recently that she can report on. We do not sign youngsters up "in advance"; they register only when they are ready to play. We then give her a book form to fill out and a number. The book form will be used to keep a record of each book she reads. The numbers allow the children to play in turn. That way, they don't have to wait in line, and the staff can call up each player on a first-come-first-served basis.

A staff member advises the child that she may report on up to two books a day. The report consists of answering some simple questions about the book, or the child may be asked to give a brief oral summary. After giving her report, the child may take one turn at the board for each book she has reported on. For better readers, a book over one hundred pages long counts as two books and results in two turns.

After the child has given her report, the book's title is written on the book form filled out earlier. The form is then filed in a box alphabetically by the child's last name. Given the large number of participants, it is important to file these forms carefully.

Now it is time for the youngster to play the game. If it's the child's first time, we explain the premise and objective of the game. Then the child chooses which of the three teams she wishes to join. (The child may choose a different team each time she plays; however, most youngsters remain loyal to one team.)

The child spins the pointer, or throws dice, to obtain a random number. The number determines how many spaces the child can move her team's character. Some of the spaces on the game path contain instructions, which may award a prize or direct the player to a side table.

If during a turn the character reaches the end of the game path, the player adds the appropriate score token to her team's scorecard.

When a youngster has reported on ten books, or five "two-turn" books (one hundred or more pages long), she is placed on the Honor Roll. She writes her name on a poster in the library, and later an Honor Roll certificate is sent to her school for presentation in class at the beginning of the upcoming school year.

When a player qualifies for the Honor Roll, she obtains an "earned" prize. This prize is chosen by drawing a colored poker chip from a jar. The honor roll prizes are slightly better than those won by chance in the game. The color of the chosen chip determines the winning prize.

In order to encourage continued reading, we have established a rule that for every additional ten books (or five two-turn books), a child may add a star after her name on the Honor Roll poster and pick another chip from the container for a prize. The idea is to create a constant incentive for the children to read more books. The small prizes awarded during the game will generate the most interest. You may want to vary the type of more advanced prizes—and the conditions under which they are awarded—according to your situation.

We have devised an additional motivation to encourage children to read Newbery winners and Newbery honor books. A youngster who reads any five of these titles earns a special ribbon. We obtain the ribbons from a company that specializes in imprinting plaques and ribbons. We have the ribbons imprinted with the words: "Newbery Award Reader, Glenview Public Library. Summer 19--". We then affix gold Newbery Medal sticky seals purchased from the American Library Association to the top of each ribbon. The ribbons are fairly inexpensive, and look very impressive with the Newbery Medal seal.

CHAPTER 2

Resources for the Project

MATERIALS The summer program requires a number of standard materials. In this chapter we will describe these materials and provide tips on how to create most of them. (See Figure 2.1.)

Physical Setup Most of the games require the following elements to be set up in the children's area:

The game board. This is the largest and most difficult element to construct. We mount ours on a twelve-by-nine-foot bulletin board, but most of the games work just as well on a large table.

The board will be the centerpiece of your program, and so should receive much attention. It is not possible to reproduce full-size game boards in this book. Instead we have created miniature sketches for each game to suggest what the finished board might look like. Exact duplication is not necessary; the specific scenes (such as volcanoes, jungles, and so forth) on the board are only suggestions, and may be shifted about with no harm done.

For detailed information on constructing your game board, see Appendix C.

Once the board has been created, the game path may be cut out of colored paper and glued to the board, or you may simply leave the path blank, painting around it as the board is created. The path should be three to four inches wide and follow a nicely convoluted route around the board. The exact route of the path is not crucial. It is only important that it does not cross over itself—unless intended by the game—and that it sooner or later arrives at its destination. We typically start our path in the lower left-hand corner of the board and end in the lower right. Use a dry marker to break the path into a series of squares.

Some of the squares are marked so as to send a player who lands on them to a side table. Occasionally this is related to the plot, as

FIGURE 2.1 Game elements for "The White Tiger of Kalimar"

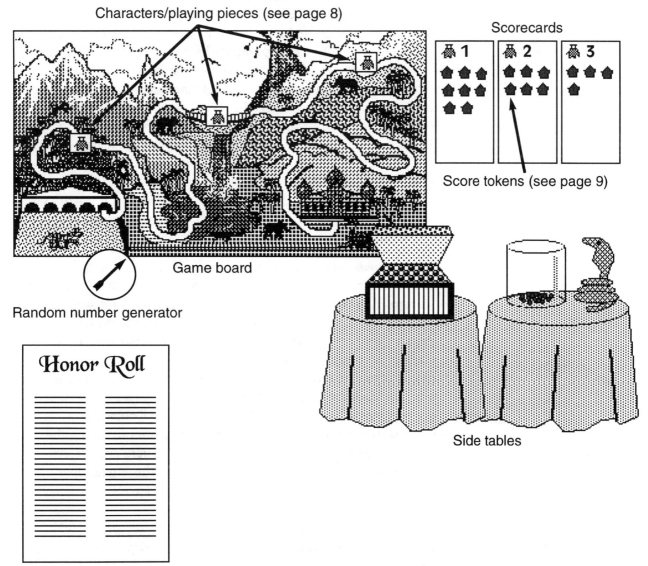

Characters/playing pieces (see page 8)

Scorecards

Score tokens (see page 9)

Game board

Random number generator

Side tables

Honor Roll

Honor Roll poster

when a player deposits a ransom jewel at one of the side tables. Usually, however, a visit to the side table allows the player to claim a prize. The number of prize squares you put onto your game path will affect the speed of the game. You will want to experiment to find the number that creates the most excitement with the fewest delays— and a reasonable drain on your prize supplies. It's best to start with a small number of prize squares first, then increase them as necessary, based on an estimate of how many prizes may be awarded each day without running out of prizes before the end of the game.

Characters. We organize the game so that participants may join any one of three teams, each represented by a different character. One team is designed to appeal to boys, another to girls, and the third to both sexes. For example, in "The Lost Library of Atlantis" one team is represented by a boy diver, another by a mermaid, and the third by a seahorse. We have found this boy-girl-animal (or creature) combination to be quite popular. Each team is represented on the game board by a distinctive playing piece. Each team also has its own scorecard, which is mounted conspicuously on the wall. Some children are fiercely loyal to one team; others change teams with each play. There are no losing individuals or teams; all contribute to a specific happy outcome in which, for example, the tiger is ransomed, the books are returned, or the aliens are defeated. It is the *team's* progress that is shown on the scorecards, not the progress of individual children.

Scorecards. These are mounted on the wall near the game board. These cards can be made from large pieces of thin cardboard or construction paper. About two by three feet is a good size. There should be one scorecard for each team, and each should have a distinctive color and bear a picture of the team's character. Each time a playing piece reaches the end of the game, the youngster whose turn it is obtains a score token for the team. For example, when a player arrives at the palace of the Phantom Maharaja in "The White Tiger of Kalimar," a plastic jewel is placed in the Cobra King's ransom jar (on a side table) while a paper token representing the jewel is placed on the scorecard for that team. There are different denominations of paper tokens. For example, "The White Tiger of Kalimar" has tokens representing 1, 10, and 100 jewels. This helps prevent swamping the scorecards with tokens.

Over the years we have learned to cover our scorecards with Con-Tact paper in advance, so that tokens backed with tape can be removed easily and replaced with larger denomination tokens.

Side tables. Some games make use of side tables. Certain squares on the game path direct the player to the side table, which is usually an occasion to receive a prize. There may be one, two, or even three tables. Any small table will do, round or square. If space is at a premium, the top of a low bookcase, a convenient shelf, windowsill, or corner of a desk will do. Each table is decorated in keeping with the game's theme. For example, in "The Lost Library of Atlantis" one of the side tables holds a small aquarium. The player uses a fishing pole with a magnet on its line to pick a metal piece from the bottom of the aquarium. The number on the bottom of the piece determines which small prize is won.

Random number generator. This can be a roulette-type wheel, a die, or a spinner you make or borrow from another game. It determines how many spaces the game piece will move along the game path. Place it as close to the game board as possible.

Playing pieces. These are paper cutouts of the game's characters, three to four inches high. The pieces are moved around the board according to the number generated. In order to make moving around the board easier, we make liberal use of Velcro. We tape a strip of Velcro across each space on the game path. Each of the three playing pieces has a corresponding piece of Velcro on its back so it can adhere to whichever square it lands on.

Score tokens. These are attached to the scorecards as the game progresses to show how many points each team has scored. They are usually cut out of paper and come in various denominations. Samples of these are provided for most of the games in this book.

Additional Elements   In addition to the furnishing for the game area, each game requires the following materials:

Book forms. These are simply records of the books each child has read. A form (usually a five-by-seven-inch card or sheet of paper) is filled out for each child when he or she registers to play the game the first time. The forms are filed alphabetically in a convenient drawer, and updated each time the child reports on a book. The book forms must be carefully maintained, since they are the records from which Honor Roll certificates will be issued.

Brochures. These are important for advertising the game. They are distributed to schools in the weeks before the game starts, and given to patrons visiting the library. Covers for the brochure for each game are included in this book.

Honor Roll certificates. Children who read enough books to make the Honor Roll (we stipulate ten books or five "two-turn" books) are presented with an Honor Roll certificate. The certificates are not given out at the library, but are mailed to the child's school and presented by the teacher during the first days of class in the fall. This public acknowledgement is enormously gratifying to the child, and helps draw attention to the library as the new school year begins. Certificates for each game are included in this book.

Coupons. Some of the prizes we award consist of coupons good for various food items at local restaurants. For example, a local pizzeria allows us to give coupons good for an individual small pizza, and a dairy bar accepts coupons for a small cone. Since this is an optional element, we have not included coupons in the book. But they are quite easy to design on your own. If possible, they should incorporate some artwork from the game in order to discourage forgery. Figure 2.2 is a sample of the kind of coupons we use.

Early in the year we arrange with businesses for the specific number of coupons they are willing to donate, and any restrictions they want to include on the coupon. For example, the pizza restaurant asked us to stipulate that the pizza could be obtained only in person, and could not be delivered. All coupons stipulate that they are not redeemable for cash, and specify a date after which they will no longer be honored. We then design a coupon unique to each business, six to a sheet. They are printed on heavy paper stock. We write consecutive numbers on them, up to the number agreed upon by the donor. Be careful to store these coupons in a locked drawer or other safe place, since they are as good as cash.

FIGURE 2.2   Sample prize coupon

Prize coupon
No.:_____

**Good for one
personal pizza**
(no anchovies)
at

The
**Acme Pizza
Emporium**

Not redeemable for cash   Expires September 30, 19__

Pleasant View Public Library 19__   Summer Reading Program

Other prizes. The choice of prizes given during your game will depend on the quantity you need and on your budget. Again we stress that the prizes may be quite simple. Bookmarks, buttons, stickers, pencils, pads of paper, keychains—all are appreciated and add to the game's excitement. Actually, even though it might be possible to obtain them through donations, expensive prizes might well be counterproductive. The real purpose of the game is to promote reading, after all, not to acquire expensive gifts.

STAFFING   These summer programs will put a heavy load on your staff. Creating and preparing the materials, listening to book reports, and guiding children through the game will consume a great deal of time. We reduced this problem by enlisting the aid of volunteers.

Our STAR (Summer Time Assisting Readers) program has been a great success in providing volunteers. Toward the end of the school year, we distribute flyers to junior high and high school classrooms asking for volunteers (we require volunteers to have completed seventh grade or higher). Students who sign up as STAR volunteers are asked to commit themselves to at least six hours over the course of the summer. The STAR volunteers do much of the registration, listen to book reports, and help the children play the board game and select prizes. We find that older children have a great deal of fun helping the younger ones this way.

STAR volunteers are given a short training program in which they are taught how the game works, the rules, and how to relate to younger children. We suggest the sorts of questions to ask, and we encourage the volunteers to maintain a lighthearted atmosphere. The book reports are not academic exercises, but are intended simply to ensure that the child has read the book. Of course, an adult member of the staff is always available to answer questions or provide assistance.

While on the floor, volunteers wear special STAR badges with their names printed on them (see Figure 2.3).

FIGURE 2.3   Volunteer badge

After performing their six or more hours of service, the volunteers are presented with a modest gift, such as a gift certificate to a local eatery. We also send a letter of thanks to the volunteers, which they may use as evidence of community service for class or scouting requirements. We have been successful at incorporating over sixty volunteers per summer as active helpers. The STAR program has also been a great success in soliciting teachers and principals from local schools to serve as volunteers for a morning or an afternoon. This strategy builds good public relations for the school and helps library and school personnel become better acquainted.

CHAPTER 3

How to Use the Materials

This book contains materials for ten games. Each includes a description of the game and artwork for the playing pieces, brochure cover, Honor Roll certificate, score tokens, and other miscellaneous graphics. You will have to create the game board itself, using the sketch included with each game as a guide. (See Appendix C for suggestions on constructing your game board.) You will also need to design any coupons to be used as prizes, although you may use any of the game artwork as part of a coupon.

Because of the many elements involved, the games will require a number of weeks or months to prepare for—especially since you will have your usual library activities to attend to as well. Scheduling the various preparations is therefore important. Appendix A presents a typical schedule such as we follow for our games.

When you decide to use a particular game, the first thing you should do is make copies of the artwork. You can make high-quality photocopies of the art pages in this book or, if you prefer to work with digital files, you can use your Web browser to download the graphics from the ALA Editions Web site. All of the artwork, with instructions for downloading it, is available at http://www.ala.org/editions/SRPFun. You can use the digital file to produce your own camera-ready output or import the image into a graphics program for modification.

When printing the villains and score tokens, use appropriately colored paper. For example, we used pink paper for the mischievous pigs in "The Case of the Baker Street Baker," and day-glow green and purple paper for the energy crystal score tokens in "Lost in Time."

Since the character playing pieces sustain the most wear and tear, you should prepare a number of copies of each to replace those that wear out. Print or copy the playing piece pages onto heavy white paper or thin card stock. Color the costumes of the characters to match the colors of their scorecards. Cut out each character, then cover it on both sides with a transparent laminate such as Con-Tact paper. Transparent package wrapping tape may also be used.

If you intend to use Velcro to attach the playing pieces to the squares on the game board, stick a piece of Velcro to the back of each piece. If you are setting the game up on a table top, glue the playing piece to a small block of wood. Both methods are illustrated in Figure 3.1.

FIGURE 3.1 Constructing the playing pieces

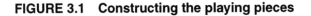

Before cutting the character out, color it, then glue the page to a piece of cardboard. Next cover the page with a transparent laminate. Cut the character out and glue a piece of Velcro to the back so that it will stick to the game board.

If your game board is on a tabletop, glue the character to a small block of wood.

In cases where the characters are human, we have attempted to include a multicultural representation. Feel free to modify or adapt these characters as needed.

The character playing pieces, villains, score tokens, and most miscellaneous art may be printed out in the library. But since the brochures and Honor Roll certificates may require hundreds of copies, you will probably want to send them to a local print shop. Before you do, add the name of your library and the dates of your program in the empty space provided on the brochure cover and Honor Roll certificate. Your printing company may be able to work with graphics files you have downloaded from the ALA Editions Web site. They may also be able to pick up art directly from these pages without damaging the book. If not, you can send them a high-quality photocopy of the art from this book to be used as camera-ready art.

The brochure cover should be printed on the bottom half of an 8½-by-11-inch sheet of paper. A list of other activities at the library may be printed, upside down, on the top half of the sheet. The rules of the game should be printed on the back side of the sheet. The idea is that when the brochure is folded in half, the cover is on the front, the rules of the game inside, and the other activities on the back (see Figure 3.2). Ask your print shop to use appropriately colored paper for the brochures and Honor Roll certificates.

Each Honor Roll certificate should be printed twice, at the top and bottom of a single 8½-by-11-inch sheet of sturdy colored paper. You can then cut each sheet in half to obtain two certificates per sheet (see Figure 3.3).

If you wish to create coupons as prizes from local businesses, see page 10 for suggestions.

You need not have everything printed at once. The brochures should be printed first, so that they may be taken to schools during class visits in the spring. The Honor Roll certificates, however, will not be needed until school starts in the fall.

Once the artwork has been assembled, you should prepare a press release to send to local newspapers that includes one of the characters or your logo. Some of the artwork and program information should also be prepared for publication in your library's newsletter or other information materials.

Although it is not essential, we like to create large posters with enlarged pictures from the game to use when we visit classes. They really help grab the students' attention.

The games that require side tables all have sketches and suggestions on how to decorate the tables.

The games in this book may be used in any order, and you may wish to start off with one of the simpler games for your first effort. Since each library differs in its facility, staffing, and clientele, you

FIGURE 3.2   Brochure format

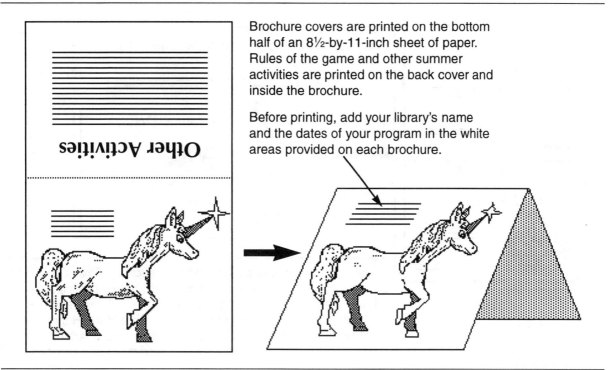

Brochure covers are printed on the bottom half of an 8½-by-11-inch sheet of paper. Rules of the game and other summer activities are printed on the back cover and inside the brochure.

Before printing, add your library's name and the dates of your program in the white areas provided on each brochure.

may need to modify some elements of the game to suit your circumstances. Reducing the number of side tables, or altering one of the characters, are examples of changes you might want to make. Most of the games allow considerable flexibility in how they are set up and played. We encourage you to add your own creative touches.

FIGURE 3.3   Honor Roll certificate

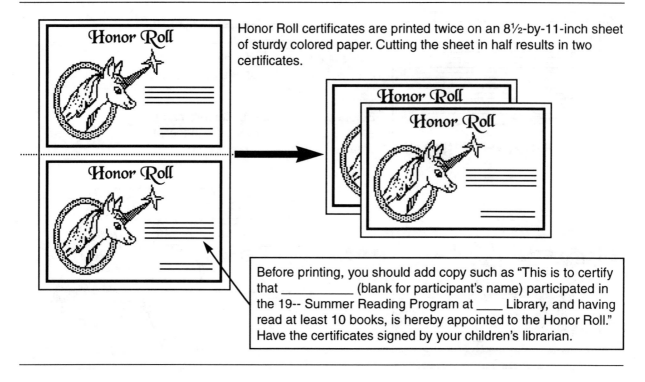

Honor Roll certificates are printed twice on an 8½-by-11-inch sheet of sturdy colored paper. Cutting the sheet in half results in two certificates.

Before printing, you should add copy such as "This is to certify that _____ (blank for participant's name) participated in the 19-- Summer Reading Program at ____ Library, and having read at least 10 books, is hereby appointed to the Honor Roll." Have the certificates signed by your children's librarian.

PART 2

Game Instructions and Graphics

The Haunted Mansion

THE GAME "The Haunted Mansion" is about a team of three ghost exterminators who remove unwanted ghosts from the Moonbright mansion. The game board is a floor plan of the mansion, with five or six rooms. Ghosts are spotted throughout the building and may be removed by one of the characters stopping in a specially marked square. There are no side tables with this game.

THE BOARD Use your imagination in designing your game board. You may use a simple overhead plan like a blueprint, with furniture, carpets, and flooring indicated by drawings or cutouts of colored paper. If you can create perspective drawings of the rooms, so much the better. Commercial board games such as Clue can provide inspiration for producing interesting floor plans. Some possible arrangements for this type of game are shown in appendix C.

This is an ideal game to set up on a tabletop. If you do use a table, you can use large dollhouse furniture for props. Doilies or scraps of fabric make excellent carpets, and you may be able to find patterned paper in hobby shops to represent wood, tile, or brick floors. This is supposed to be a deserted house, so worn carpet, seedy furniture, and cobwebs are the rule.

The game path should begin at the front door and wind its way through the series of rooms. Each character begins at the front door and completes a trip around the path through the entire house before returning to the front door and starting again. Each room is populated with several ghosts. When a character stops in a specially marked square, one of the ghosts is removed from that room using the "ghost nabber," and placed in the "ectoplasmic vault." Record the capture on that character's scorecard.

GAME 1   The Haunted Mansion: Game board

Game board for The Haunted Mansion is the floor plan of the house. The game path travels through all the rooms, returning to the entrance hall.

The paper cutout ghosts are scattered throughout the mansion, ready to be picked up by the player landing on the appropriate square.

This game is ideal for setting up on a tabletop, in which case cardboard walls and doll furniture may be used to furnish the mansion. Pieces of fabric or construction paper may be used for rugs and curtains.

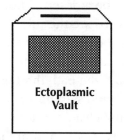

Ectoplasmic Vault

A small cardboard box with a plastic or cellophane window should be set up near the game board. Cut a slot in the top to receive the captured ghosts. See page 25 for instructions.

THE CHARACTERS The characters consist of a boy, a girl, and a dog. We called the boy Wild Bill Batfree. He is shown with his electronic spirit-detection probe. The girl, Sally Spectre, wields an ectoplasmic vacuum and speeds around on jet-powered skates. "Woofer the Wonder Dog" flies through the game with his helicopter backpack, equipped with ghost radar.

You will need lots of ghosts. Make multiple copies of the sheet of ghosts included here, or make your own using a similar design. Remember to glue a paper clip or straight pin inside each ghost as you fold the two halves together. If your game is on a tabletop you will need to provide bases so the ghosts will stand upright. The bases may be made of balsa wood (available at craft and hobby stores) and should be provided with a slot loose enough so that the ghost may be easily lifted out by the magnetic ghost nabber. If your game board is on the wall, you will need to install little hooks on the backs of the ghosts and hang them from eyelets screwed into the board.

Use more ghost cutouts to make score tokens to hang on the scorecards. Mark these in 1, 10, and 100-ghost "denominations."

SIDE TABLES None. Since there are no side tables, various squares on the game board should award prizes directly. (For example: "Choose one food prize coupon.")

TECHNICAL STUFF The "ghost nabber" is simply a thin dowel, about a foot long, with a magnet glued to the end. Paint the dowel a bright color or wrap colored tape around it, barber-pole fashion. Your "ectoplasmic vault" can be created from a small box (we used a cigar box). Cut a window into the front of the box and tape colored cellophane over the opening to add drama. The vault may be located in one of the rooms of the house, or may be placed like a jail in some nearby location. Wherever it is, you will have to cheat occasionally and remove some of the ghosts to restock the house. This is best done after hours or just before the library opens! You may need to experiment with how many ghosts to have in the house, and how many squares to mark for capturing a ghost. You need to have as many captures as possible to keep the game interesting, yet not run out of ghosts during the course of the day.

GAME 1   The Haunted Mansion: Characters

HAUNTINGS R-US

Wild Bill Batfree

Sally Spectre

Woofer the
Wonder Dog

GAME 1   The Haunted Mansion: Ghosts

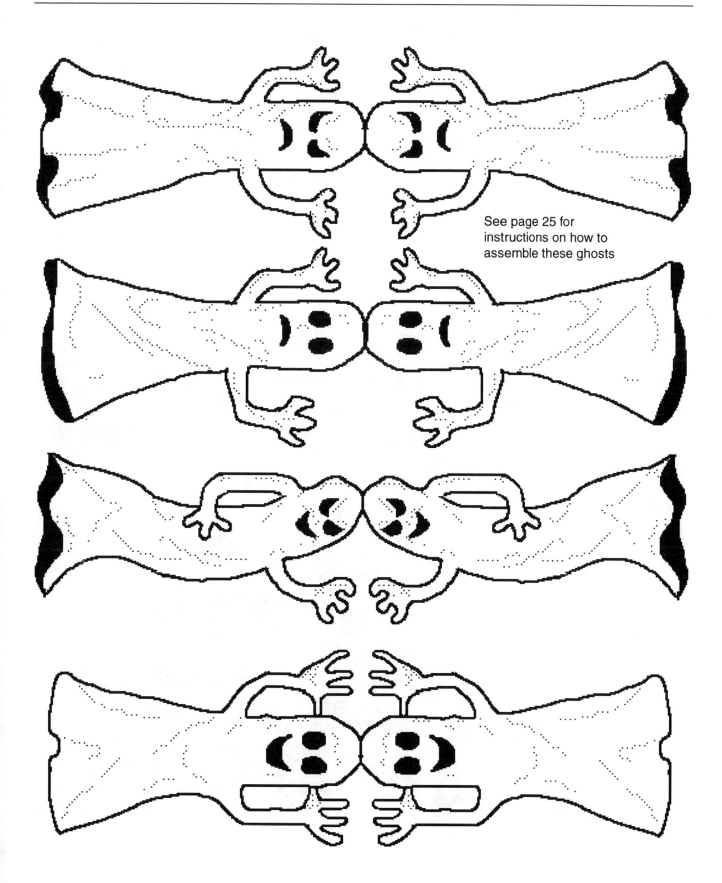

See page 25 for instructions on how to assemble these ghosts

FINISHING TOUCHES   Cobwebs and ghost cutouts may be scattered around the children's area in the library. Skeletons, ghosts, and spider webs, adapted from Halloween decorations, may be used to decorate the area too, but in order to avoid a clash of seasons, avoid such elements as pumpkins, black cats, or witches. There are spooky sound-effect tapes available that might be played softly in the background. Such extras will depend on how much time you have and how much your staff can tolerate constantly repeating sound effects.

At the end of the program, the team that has captured the most ghosts—as revealed by the scorecards—wins. Leave the ghost-free house in place for a week or more, so that visitors will have an ample chance to view the results. You might even want to install a smiling paper-doll family in the house, now that the unwanted guests are gone!

GAME 1   The Haunted Mansion: Brochure cover

Ghosts have taken over the old Moonbright mansion, and the ghost squad has been called! Join the excitement at the library this summer, and help clear out...

The Haunted Mansion!

Hauntings R-Us

GAME 1   The Haunted Mansion: Ghost assembly instructions and Honor Roll certificate

Hide a paper clip or straight pin between the halves of the paper ghosts—this allows them to be picked up by the "ghost nabber"—a stick with a small magnet attached to the end.

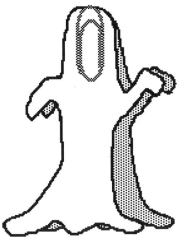

On wall-mounted games, tape small hooks to the back of each ghost. Hang the ghosts from small eyelets screwed into the bulletin board. This allows the ghosts to be easily lifted by the magnetic wand.

On a tabletop, slip the ghosts into a groove cut into small blocks of wood. Make sure the groove is wide enough to allow the ghost to slip out easily.

Ghosts are deposited in the nearby ectoplasmic vault (a small box with a slot cut into the top and a window made from colored cellophane).

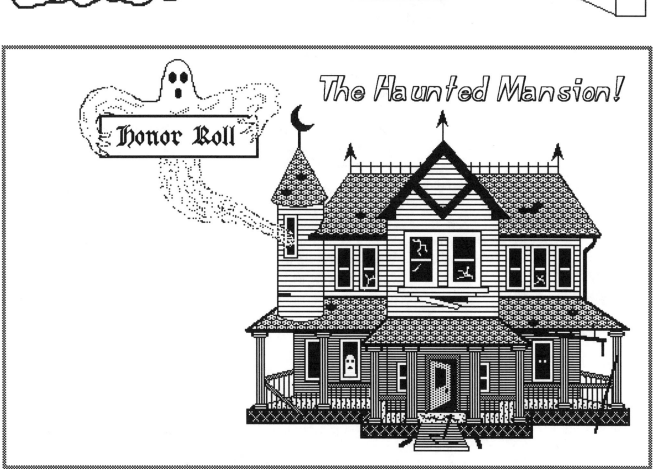

GAME 2

....

Read-errific Runaround

THE GAME   This game represents a marathon race, with three runners competing for the most successful trips around the track.

THE BOARD   The general design of the game board is suggested by the brochure cover. The game path is a basic oval, but with three "detours" leading to some strange areas. A character who lands on the square where a detour branches off must roll the pointer again. Odd numbers must take the detour, even numbers continue straight ahead.

The three detours are through Pirates Cove, the Land of the Dinosaurs, and the Mummy's Tomb. Feel free to change any or all of these to areas that might be of more interest to your patrons. Again, construction of the game board may be as elaborate or as simple as your resources allow. Pirates Cove features a skull-shaped mountain and a body of water with a pirate ship on it. These settings can be constructed as simple paper cutouts, as paintings, or as papier-mâché sculptures. Blue cellophane makes a nice lake. You may be able to find a half-model of a sailing ship to use as the pirate ship. Or you can make one using cardboard for the hull, dowels for masts, and white paper sails. Just don't forget the Jolly Roger skull-and-crossbones flag!

The Land of the Dinosaurs may be dressed up with papier-mâché or Styrofoam volcanoes, plastic plants for jungles, and plastic dinosaur models available from toy stores. Cutouts from magazines work fine too. Use cotton puffs—died black, if possible—to provide smoke from the volcanoes. White cotton puffs may be stretched across the trees to suggest fog. Use green Easter-basket "grass" for vines and clear cellophane or Christmas tinsel streams to suggest waterfalls. Be sure to exaggerate the sharp mountain edges and steep cliffs. Use dark blue, purple, or brown paper, set off by lurid orange and yellow fire, for the volcano.

GAME 2   Read-errific Runaround: Brochure cover (which is also the game board sketch)

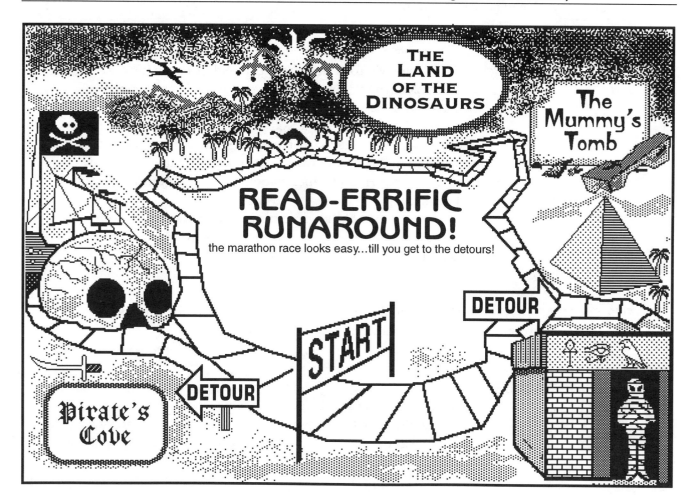

GAME 2   Read-errific Runaround: Side tables 1 and 3

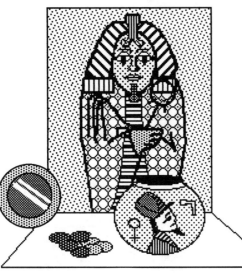

Some squares in the dinosaur area direct players to this dinosaur "nest," made of rocks, straw and plastic eggs. A paper cutout or painting of a dinosaur completes the setup. Players pick an egg and turn it over to discover the number determining their prize.

Some squares in the Mummy's Tomb area direct players to this table. The color of a poker chip drawn from the Egyptian "urn" determines the prize. The urn is a fishbowl painted with Egyptian symbols. Background is a travel poster.

The Mummy's Tomb may be a pyramid or rectangular box made from styrofoam and painted yellow, or cut out from sandpaper. Decorate with lots of hieroglyphics in bright colors. For a three-dimensional mummy, wrap a Ken or action-figure doll in thin strips of cotton sheeting. Age by staining the figure with brown water colors or tea. Surround the tomb with a desert of sandpaper (or yellow construction paper) and paper cutouts (or plastic models) of camels and palm trees.

The center area of the game board may be decorated with flags and bleacher seats to suggest a stadium, or with grass and trees to suggest a cross-country race.

THE CHARACTERS   Participants in this marathon are three whimsical creatures: Speed E. Gator, Indy Inchworm, and Olivia Ostrich.

SIDE TABLES   We used three side tables with this game, each decorated to match a detour area on the game board. Each table stood next to a wall or pillar. The Egyptian table was covered with a sheet of sandpaper. A sheet of yellow paper on the wall was painted with hieroglyphics in bright colors. If you can find a travel poster with the mask of King Tut or a view of the pyramids, so much the better. On the table was a bowl made from a small aquarium. The bowl was also painted with hieroglyphics, and filled with different colored poker chips. Each child who landed on a specially marked square in the Mummy's Tomb area was brought to the Egyptian table and allowed to reach into the bowl and draw out a chip. The color of the chip determined the prize.

The Pirates Cove table was decorated with nautical props. A fishing net was tacked to the wall and draped down over the table. Here is another good place for a Jolly Roger flag. A plastic cutlass and plastic skull add to the atmosphere. On the table we placed a small trunk to serve as a sea chest. Inside the chest were gold coins made of milk chocolate covered with gold paper. You might give away the coins themselves, or write numbers on them to refer to other prizes. Plastic toy jewelry may also be used to add interest to the chest.

The Land of the Dinosaurs table consisted of a circle of black stones with some straw in the middle to represent a dinosaur nest. The long-necked head of a brontosaurus was cut out of paper and taped to the wall next to the table. Inside the nest we used old L'Eggs pantyhose containers painted grey. Large Easter eggs or even baseball-sized plastic balls could also be used. A number was painted on each egg, which was then placed face-down in the nest. A child landing on the proper square in the Land of the Dinosaurs would be taken to the table to pick up one of the eggs and receive a prize according to the number.

FINISHING TOUCHES

The three scorecards represent each racer, of course. You might want to coordinate the colors used on the characters' costumes with the colors used for the scorecards. For example, you might color Speed E. Gator's outfit blue, and use a blue sheet of paper for his scorecard. Use checkered flags for the score tokens in 1, 10, and 100 denominations for each crossing of the finish line. These, of course, may easily be made from paper and reproduced in great numbers with a photocopier.

GAME 2 Read-errific Runaround: Characters

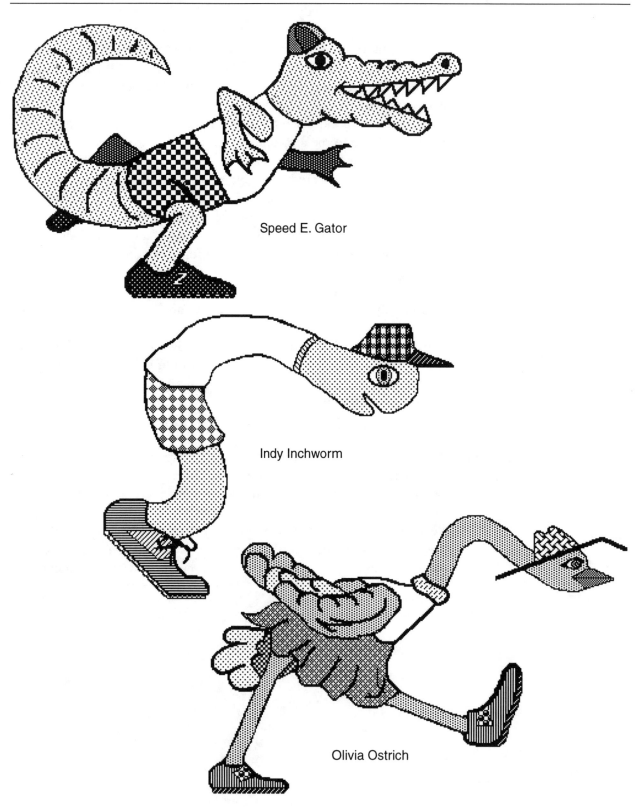

Speed E. Gator

Indy Inchworm

Olivia Ostrich

GAME 2 Read-errific Runaround: Side table 2 and Honor Roll certificate

Special squares in the Pirate's Cove area direct players to this table. An old trunk or box represents a treasure chest. Decorate with such props as a fishnet, seashells or a dried starfish. Chocolate or plastic "gold" coins and fake jewelry make up the treasure. Players pick a coin and check its underside to find the number that determines their prize.

READ-ERRIFIC RUNAROUND!
Honor Roll Certificate

GAME 2   Read-errific Runaround: Score tokens

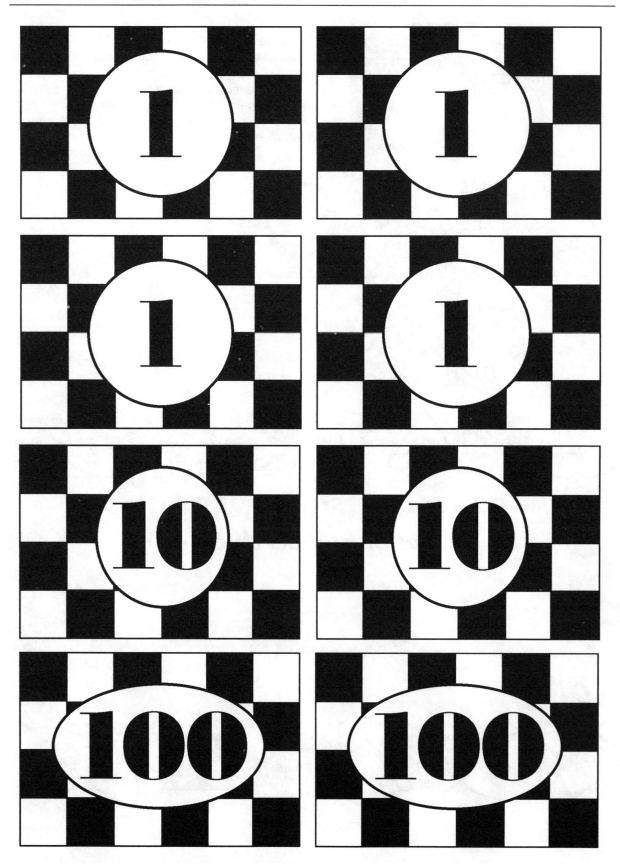

The Quest for the Golden Unicorns

THE GAME   This fantasy adventure takes place in a mythic landscape. A group of nasty trolls has kidnapped a herd of golden unicorns from Morningstar Castle. Three adventurers set off to rescue them and capture the offending trolls.

THE BOARD   You can let your imagination run wild for the game board. Anything from a realistic landscape to a wild pattern of colors and textures would make a fine background. Colored construction paper, colored foil, small branches, sponges, lichens, and plastic plants are ideal materials. Except for the area around Morningstar Castle, try to keep the overall tone of the board dark, using deep purples, forest greens, and brown. This will allow the brilliant colors of the characters, unicorns, and trolls to stand out. Place Morningstar Castle in the lower left-hand corner of the game board. Make the castle from Styrofoam sheets or painted cardboard. Use soft pastel colors for the walls, and don't forget to provide lots of turrets and flags. Glue glitter particles to the castle to give it a fairy-tale look. Create a large "pasture" of green grass around the castle for the unicorns as they are "rescued."

Put the trolls' castle in the upper right-hand corner of the board. The land around the troll castle should be grim and barren looking, with bare trees and rocks. Attach numerous paper cutout trolls to the board throughout this area.

The castle itself should be crude-looking, as if made from large, irregular stones. There should be a gate in the front of the troll castle, with bars like a prison door. Use thin wooden dowels, or thin strips of black tape on a sheet of clear plastic, to make the gate. The gate should be hinged so that it can be opened, and behind it you should have a container capable of holding a number of the paper unicorn cutouts.

GAME 3   The Quest for the Golden Unicorns: Game board and side tables

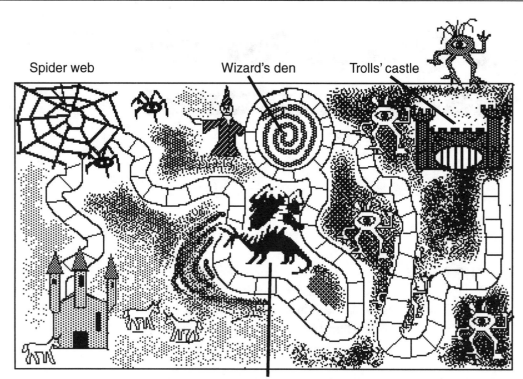

Spider web   Wizard's den   Trolls' castle

Morningstar Castle   Dragon's lair

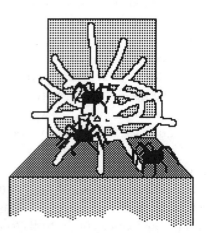

Players directed to this table from the spider web section of the game board pick a prize by looking for a number on the underside of a rubber spider. The web for this table may be made from white yarn, or simply painted on cardboard. Cobwebs from a spray can, and cotton puff "egg sacs" can be used to add atmosphere.

The dragon's lair is simply a ring of stones enclosing a group of plastic eggs. The eggs may be painted gold or silver to make them more magical. Numbers concealed on the underside of each egg reveal the nature of the prize. The dragon may be a simple cardboard or paper cutout or papier-mâché painted with features. Flat Philippine lantern seashells may be used as dragon scales instead of the eggs.

The game path should connect the two castles, of course in the most roundabout way possible. As usual, there are a number of traps and pitfalls along the way. One is a giant spider web. Set up the web next to the game path. Just paint it on the background, or better yet, make it out of white yarn for a three-dimensional effect. Populate the web with a few nasty rubber toy spiders. When players land on specially marked squares near the web, they are directed to the spider side table to select a prize.

Another hot spot along the game path is the dragon's lair. A rough oval of purple construction paper and a black paper cutout of a dragon are all that is required here. When a character lands on a specially marked square near the dragon lair, the player is sent to the dragon side table for a prize.

As the game path passes through the troll area of the board, there should be a number of squares which state that the player has captured a troll. When a character lands on one of these squares, a cutout troll is removed from the game board and attached to the scorecard for that player's team. You will want to make up a number of troll cutouts with the numbers 10 and 100 written on them. These can take the place of an equivalent number of single trolls on the scorecards to avoid overcrowding. The last square of the game path should be at the door to the troll castle. The player who lands there gets to open the door and free one of the unicorns. This unicorn should be placed on the green pasture surrounding Morningstar Castle. A token representing a unicorn should then be placed on that character's scorecard. Use additional cutout paper unicorns for these tokens.

Once a unicorn has been rescued, the character is returned to Morningstar Castle to start again.

THE CHARACTERS

The characters consist of Queen Electra, the Scarlet Knight, and the Elf King. (Of course, you may give them any names you wish.) Choose distinctive colors for each character's costume, and use the same colors to identify that character's scorecard. You will need to print up many copies of the unicorn sheet on gold-colored paper. The same is true for the sheet of trolls, only this time use a variety of neon-toned paper like chartreuse, fuschia, hot pink, or violet. Allow plenty of time for volunteers to cut out all the unicorns and trolls!

GAME 3   The Quest for the Golden Unicorns: The Scarlet Knight and brochure cover

icked trolls have kidnapped the herd of golden unicorns that protects Morningstar Castle. Now nasty spiders, dragons and trolls are invading the kingdom. Three heroes will attempt to capture the trolls and free the unicorns. Join them at the library this summer and share the excitement of…

The Quest for the Golden Unicorns

GAME 3   The Quest for the Golden Unicorns: The Elf King, Queen Electra, and Honor Roll certificate

SIDE TABLES

There are two side tables. The spider web table should include a large web, either painted on black paper or made of white yarn. The web should be populated with toy rubber spiders and seven or eight "egg sacs" made from cotton balls. Glue different colored dots to the cotton balls, then attach the cotton balls to the web so that the colored dots cannot be seen. A player directed to this table lifts one of the cotton balls. The colored dot determines which prize is won. Rather than using "egg sacs," you could place colored dots or prize numbers on the undersides of the spiders.

The dragon side table represents a dragon's nest. Attach a paper cutout of a dragon's neck and head to the wall as a background. A circle of rocks forms the nest, with cellophane Easter-basket "grass" as filling. Multicolored plastic eggs complete the picture. Write a number on each egg, then place the egg number-side down in the nest. Players directed to this table pick up an egg and look at the number to claim their prize.

TECHNICAL STUFF

After hours, you will have to restock the game board with trolls to replace those that have been captured. (You may need to add more unicorn prisoners to the troll castle as well.) In the final days of the game, gradually allow the number of trolls on the game board to diminish until there are no more at game's end.

FINISHING TOUCHES

To reinforce the theme of this game, the children's area of the library may be decorated with any items appropriate to the theme, such as posters of castles, suits of armor, swords, and coats of arms.

GAME 3   The Quest for the Golden Unicorns: Trolls

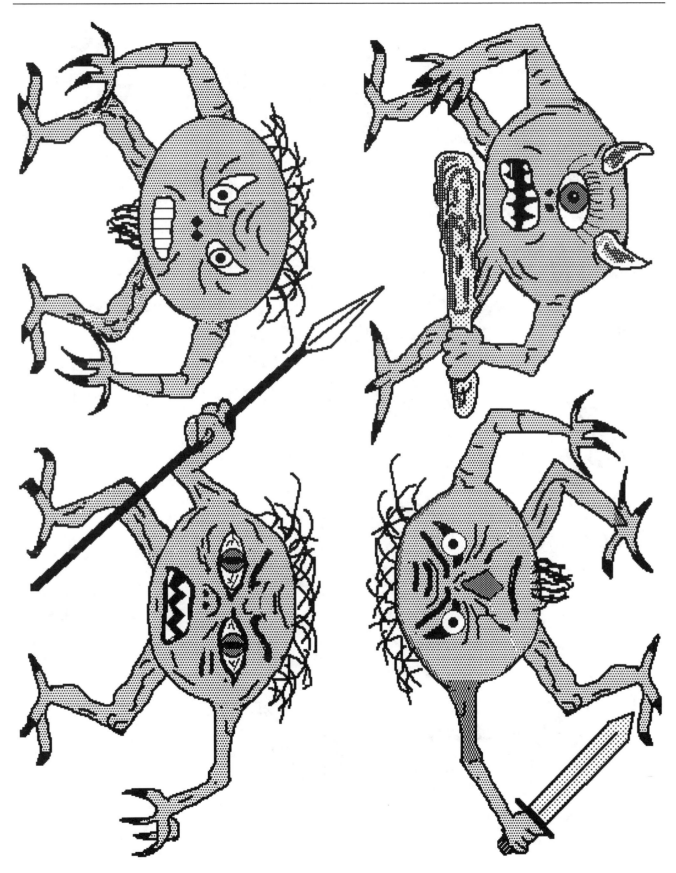

GAME 3 The Quest for the Golden Unicorns: Unicorns

The Lost City of the Aztecs

THE GAME   This game has an archaeological theme. An earthquake in Central America has revealed an enormous cave, inside of which rests a golden city built by the ancient Aztecs. Three teams of archaeologists will attempt to dismantle the golden city and reassemble it outside the cave before another earthquake buries it forever.

THE BOARD   The game board consists of a thick jungle and a cave, with a game path that weaves around the board until it reaches the city inside the cave. Include scenery such as mountains, lots of greenery, waterfalls, swamps, and volcanoes on the jungle part of the board. Green and purple paper may be used for the trees and mountains. Sheets of clear plastic or cellophane can represent streams, lakes, and waterfalls. Dark purple or brown construction paper forms a good background for the cave. Stalactites and stalagmites can be cut from construction paper and cardboard. Add some rubber (or black construction paper) bats to the upper part of the cave, and some spray-can spider webs here and there.

The city (actually a single Aztec temple pyramid) should be constructed out of cardboard covered with gold-colored foil or paper. You may use the building shown on the brochure cover as a guide or consult the numerous children's books on Aztec culture for ideas on the design and decorations of these temples. Use dry markers or strips of black paper or tape to add architectural details. Make the city in three separate pieces that can fit together to form the whole. This allows the city to be gradually taken apart during the course of the game. If the game runs six weeks, for example, you would remove one section of the city every two weeks. These sections should be stored somewhere until the game is over.

GAME 4   The Lost City of the Aztecs: Game board

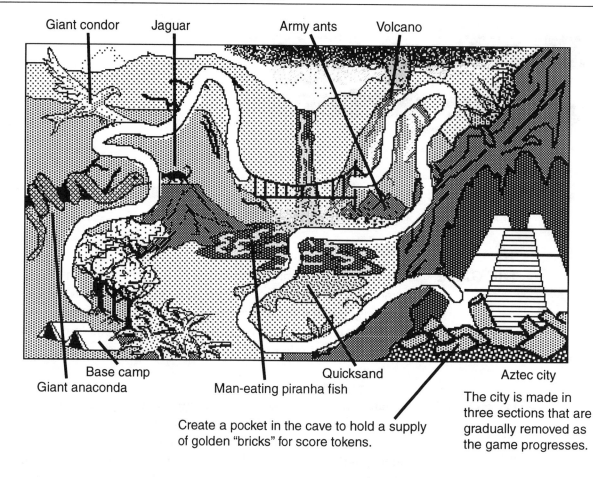

Giant condor   Jaguar   Army ants   Volcano

Base camp
Giant anaconda   Man-eating piranha fish   Quicksand   Aztec city

Create a pocket in the cave to hold a supply of golden "bricks" for score tokens.

The city is made in three sections that are gradually removed as the game progresses.

A nice (and optional) finishing touch

At the end of the game, you might want to show the city reassembled. (After all, that was the idea behind removing the city from the cave in the first place.) That can be done by gluing the three sections of the city back onto the game board somewhere outside the cave. Another approach would be to create another scene near the game board and reassemble the city there. This second scene consists simply of a few pieces of colored paper. You can wait till the game is over and create this scene all at once, or you can create the scene at the same time as the game board, and as each section of the city is removed from the cave, you can paste it on the second scene.

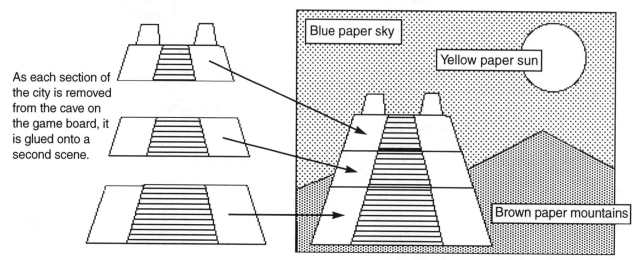

As each section of the city is removed from the cave on the game board, it is glued onto a second scene.

Blue paper sky

Yellow paper sun

Brown paper mountains

Create a pocket close to the city that can hold a number of gold paper "bricks." These are the score tokens. When a player reaches the lost city, one brick is taken out of the pocket and placed on that player's scorecard. The score tokens—simply rectangles of gold-colored construction paper—may be made in great quantities with a guillotine cutter. Use a dry marker to write the number 1 on most of the bricks. You will also want to make bricks in 10 and 100 denominations to avoid overcrowding the scorecards.

THE CHARACTERS

The three characters are: Ruiz Roho, Betty Blanco, and Azul the Blue Coyote. Their costumes should be colored primarily in red, white, and blue, respectively. Of course the scorecards should match the colors of each character.

SIDE TABLES

Certain squares on the game path should direct players to one of two side tables. Each of these tables provides a chance for a prize award. One table may be decorated in a Mexican motif. Cover the table with a serape or other colorful cloth. Decorate with such items as a sombrero, castanets, maracas, a wooden flute, or ethnic dolls. A number taped to the underside of each item reveals which prize has been won.

The second table should have an archaeological motif. Cover the table with burlap or canvas, and prop it with such things as a pith helmet, trowel, small hammer, magnifying glass, whisk broom, compass, camping equipment (battered vacuum jug, tin cups, and pans), or work gloves. Fill a metal pan with smooth stones—each stone having a number taped to the underside which corresponds to a prize.

FINISHING TOUCHES

At the end of the summer, you can simply end the game by counting all the bricks on the scorecards and leaving it at that. But a nice touch would be to actually show the city reassembled outside the cave. You could simply glue the three sections of the temple that were removed during the game back onto the game board, but outside the cave.

Another approach would be to create another outdoor scene on a wall near the game board. A simple sand-and-sky scene can be created using a large sheet of blue paper for the sky, and adding a strip of yellow paper or sand paper along the bottom to suggest a desert location. Glue an orange paper circle to the sky to represent the sun. Reassemble the city on this scene and leave it on exhibit for a week or so to confirm the happy ending to the game.

GAME 4   The Lost City of the Aztecs: Characters

Ruiz Roho   Betty Blanco

Azul the Blue Coyote

GAME 4   The Lost City of the Aztecs: Miscellaneous art and brochure cover

An earthquake in Central America has uncovered a cave containing a fabulous city of gold, built by Aztec Indians hundreds of years ago. Three teams of adventurers will try to take apart the city and rebuild it outside the cave—before another earthquake buries it forever.

Come to the library this summer
and help save...

The LOST CITY of the AZTECS

GAME 4 **The Lost City of the Aztecs: Miscellaneous Art and Honor Roll certificate**

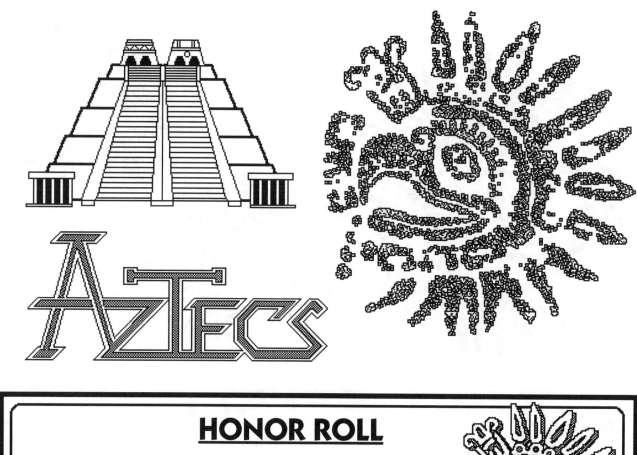

The Monster Bash

THE GAME   The monsters in the old house on the hill are having a party, and we are invited to join three of the guests in a friendly competition for goodie bags.

THE BOARD   The game board represents the interior of a decrepit mansion. You may create an overhead floor plan (it may be possible to recycle the floor plan from "The Haunted Mansion" here), or a side view of the house, complete with attic and cellar. The board should not be too grim looking, but should have a whimsical tone. Contrast stone walls with gay party streamers, hang Japanese lanterns over the tombstones in the garden, put bunches of balloons in the main hall, have candles glowing everywhere. There is no need to strive for a realistic look. Rooms can be represented by squares of wildly colored construction paper. Cut out different colored paper to represent doors and windows and paste them to the walls. Walls, doors, and windows should be a little misshapen, with corners not quite square, or tilted a bit out of line. Scraps of cloth can be glued on to represent drapes and carpets. Bizarre wallpapers can be created with foil wrapping papers. Pictures of odd-looking furniture and tables laden with food may be cut from magazines or painted.

    The game path should begin at the front door, pass through all the rooms, and end either back at the front door or at the back door. Of course, when one of the characters reaches the last square, it is returned to the first square to start over.

    People the house with a host of "monstrous" party guests. These can be a wild assortment of figures you paint yourself, along with cutouts from magazines and comic books. Science fiction and horror movie fan magazines can supply a wealth of inspiration (and pictures to cut out, too) for these characters. Be careful not to choose charac-

GAME 5   The Monster Bash: Game board

Pin the Tail on the Dragon

The Maze

Bobbing for Bats   "Hot" Scotch

ters that might frighten children; look for goofy characters rather than scary ones. The sillier the monster bash appears, the better the kids will like it. Since it is the wrong season, you will want to avoid anything that suggests Halloween, so witches, black cats, and skeletons are not invited.

Scattered throughout the house, and adjacent to the game path, should be a number of party games. These should be variations on familiar games, with a "monstrous" twist. Here are some of the ones we came up with: "Bobbing for Bats" (a washtub filled with water in which bats are seen floating), "Pin the Tail on the Dragon" (a picture of a tail-less dragon is shown taped to the wall, with numerous tails pinned both to the picture and to the wall nearby), "Hot Scotch" (a hop-scotch grid is shown on the floor, with each square in flames). You can probably think of many more. When a player lands on a specially marked square next to one of these games, that player's team is awarded a goodie bag, and a goodie bag token is placed on the scorecard for that character. The team with the most goodie bags at the end of the summer program is the winner.

THE CHARACTERS

The three characters are: Frankie Stein, a juvenile version of Mary Shelley's monster; Elmira, a juvenile version of TV horror movie hostesses; and Furp, a juvenile of indeterminate species.

SIDE TABLE

With this game we used only one side table. Ours made use of a wheel of fortune we salvaged from another game. Players directed to the side table from the game board spun the wheel and received the prize under the pointer. But you can use almost any game as the basis for your side table. A checkerboard is ideal. Cover the table with a dark cloth and prop the table with a thoroughly corroded metal candelabra festooned with fake spider webs, or use pewter cups or steins. Sprinkle a few pieces of colored confetti on the table and tape a couple of party balloons to the wall nearby. Place the checkerboard on the table and tape a number to the bottom of each checker on the board (you need to place only a few checkers on the board). Have the player choose a checker and turn it over to determine his or her prize.

GAME 5   The Monster Bash: Frankie Stein and brochure cover

Frankie Stein

GAME 5   The Monster Bash: Furp, Elmira, and Honor Roll certificate

GAME 5   The Monster Bash: Goodie bag score tokens (1)

GAME 5   The Monster Bash: Score tokens (10, 100)

GAME 6

....

The White Tiger of Kalimar

THE GAME This game takes place in India. The cub of a rare white tiger has been kidnapped by the Cobra King. The King demands a tank full of jewels as ransom. In order to ransom the cub, three teams of adventurers will travel to the remote palace of the Phantom Maharaja. The Maharaja has promised to give one jewel to each person who successfully completes the hazardous journey to his door. In the course of the game, each character travels from the Kalimar Game Preserve to the Maharaja's palace, obtains a jewel and places it in the Cobra King's tank, then returns to the starting square to begin again.

THE BOARD Inspiration for all the artwork in the game—especially landscapes and architecture—can be obtained from issues of *National Geographic,* travel magazines and brochures, and encyclopedias. Travel agents in your area may be able to supply travel posters for India that may be used as decorations in the children's department.

The game board should represent the enormously varied landscape of the Indian subcontinent. Jungles, mountains, rivers, caves, deserts, swamps—almost anything may be included. Colored construction paper is, again, the background material of choice. Styrofoam or cardboard can add dimensionality where desired, and clear plastic over blue paper can suggest water. Animals such as tigers, elephants, crocodiles, birds, and snakes—whether drawings or photographs—should be scattered liberally over the landscape. Except for the Kalimar Game Preserve where the game begins, and the Phantom Maharaja's palace, where it ends, buildings should be kept to a minimum. The odd decaying temple or statue may be added for atmosphere. The game board diagram hints at some of the possible elements and hazards you might use. The monkey jungle includes squares that direct players to the monkey side table. Most other prizes

GAME 6 The White Tiger of Kalimar: Game board, Davi Tikki Tavi playing piece and scorecard picture

Monkey jungle   Rope bridge   Volcano   Kalimar desert

Kalimar Game Preserve   Crocodile lake   Kalimar Railway (optional)

Quicksand pool   Phantom Maharaja's Palace

Davi Tikki Tavi

Playing piece   Scorecard picture

are awarded simply by landing on an appropriately marked square. The rope bridge may be a drawing or may be constructed out of string. Sandpaper makes fine deserts, and chopped-up green yarn can add depth to the vegetation. A few rubber snakes and insects wouldn't hurt. The Maharaja's palace should be a little spooky looking. Make it from purple and brown construction paper, and add yellow windows. If you can show it partially in ruins, so much the better. When we built our game board, the train that runs from the Maharaja's palace back to the Game Preserve was deemed too complicated and was dropped. After reaching the palace, playing pieces were simply moved to the starting square again. But we like the train artwork, so we are including it in case you would like to use it. Feel free to ignore it, or perhaps use it in some other game.

THE CHARACTERS

The characters in this game consist of Princess Sari, Prince Raj, and Davi Tikki Tavi, a mongoose. The playing pieces show them riding on elephants, and we have included larger pictures of their faces for use on the scorecards.

SIDE TABLES

There are three side tables, but only one, the monkey table, is used for prize distribution. Use a large stuffed monkey or a paper cutout, with perhaps a tree branch for it to sit on. On the table itself place a stack of four or five coconuts, each with a number painted on it. The coconuts should, of course, be stacked so that the numbers are not visible. When a player lands on an appropriate square on the game board, he goes to the side table and chooses one of the coconuts. The prize is determined by the number painted on it. If coconuts are not available in your area, plastic or wax bananas may be used.

The Phantom Maharaja's treasure chest, filled with plastic jewels, sits on the second side table. The chest must contain enough jewels to fill the Cobra King's tank. These may be obtained from toy or novelty stores, as well as some craft shops. Beads or marbles may be used in a pinch. A jewel box or decorated cardboard box may be used for the chest. When a player arrives at the Maharaja's palace, he is allowed to choose one jewel from the chest and place it in the Cobra King's tank (on side table 3). A paper score token representing a jewel is placed on that player's scorecard at the same time. The Phantom Maharaja's table should be covered with bright Indian print fabric (available from fabric stores) and decorated with Indian-theme props, such as brass lamps, incense burners, and elephants.

The third table represents the Cobra King's den. This should be decorated with rocks and plastic greens, but should also include some brilliant fabric and the trappings of royalty, such as brass goblets and candlesticks. You can use a large rubber snake for the King if you can find one, or make one from papier-mâché. A large photograph or drawing of a cobra can also be used, taped on the wall adjacent to the table. We placed a clear plastic cylindrical fish tank on the table to hold the jewels. Any clear container will do. The idea is to be able to see the level of jewels rising as the game progresses. (You may have to "cheat" now and then and remove some of the jewels after hours if the container threatens to fill up before the game is over for the summer.)

FINISHING TOUCH You may wish to show the tiger cub as prisoner during the course of the game. Depending on how elaborate you want to be, this could be anything from a stuffed toy tiger in a cardboard "cage" to a drawing or photograph hung behind black paper "bars."

GAME 6   The White Tiger of Kalimar: Princess Sari playing piece and scorecard picture, brochure cover

Princess Sari

Playing piece

Scorecard picture

The wicked Cobra King has kidnapped a white tiger cub from its home in the Kalimar Game Preserve. Three teams of adventurers will try to gather the ransom and return the tiger to its home. Come to the library this summer and help rescue…

Property of the
Cobra King
KEEP OUT!

The
White
Tiger
of Kalimar

GAME 6   The White Tiger of Kalimar: Prince Raj playing piece and scorecard picture, Honor Roll certificate

Prince Raj

Playing piece

Scorecard picture

GAME 6   The White Tiger of Kalimar: Side tables

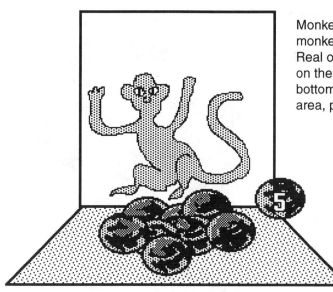

Monkey nest. This table should be propped with a monkey—a stuffed toy, a drawing, or paper cutout. Real or cutout branches may be added. Coconuts on the table have prize numbers taped to the bottom side. If coconuts are not available in your area, plastic fruit may be used.

Players who land on the Phantom Maharaja's palace come to this table to obtain a ransom jewel. A fancy box or chest filled with plastic jewels is all that is required. Indian-style print cloth, brass bowls, elephants, or candlesticks will add atmosphere.

The jewels that are obtained from the Phantom Maharaja are placed in a container at this side table. A toy stuffed or rubber snake, or just a drawing or picture can be decorated with a crown, fancy draperies, and other royal accessories. A clear container—aquarium or bowl—is used to hold the jewelry. (You may have to remove some of the jewels after hours to prevent the container from filling up before the end of the summer.)

GAME 6   The White Tiger of Kalimar: Score tokens

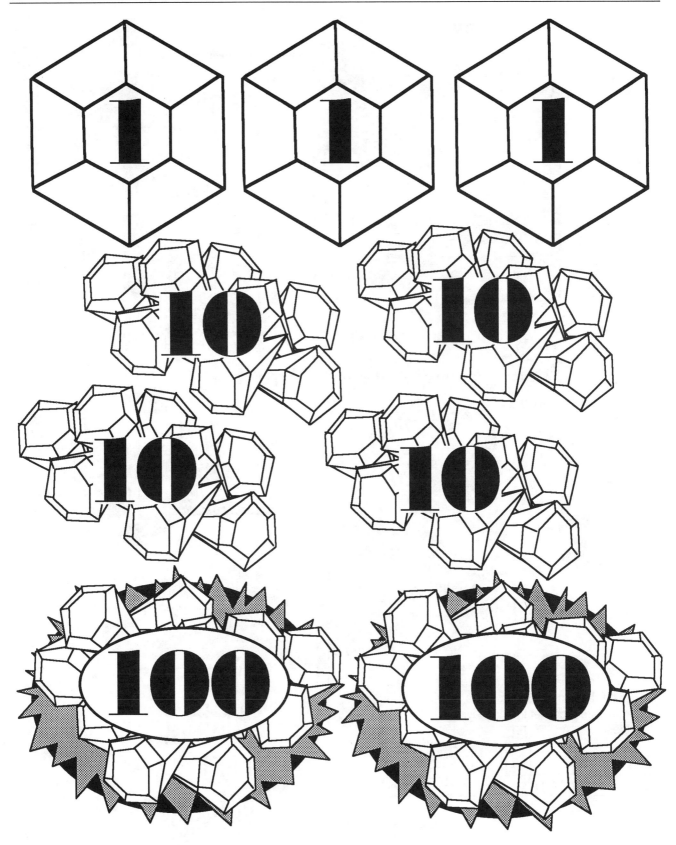

GAME 6   The White Tiger of Kalimar: Train and art for logo

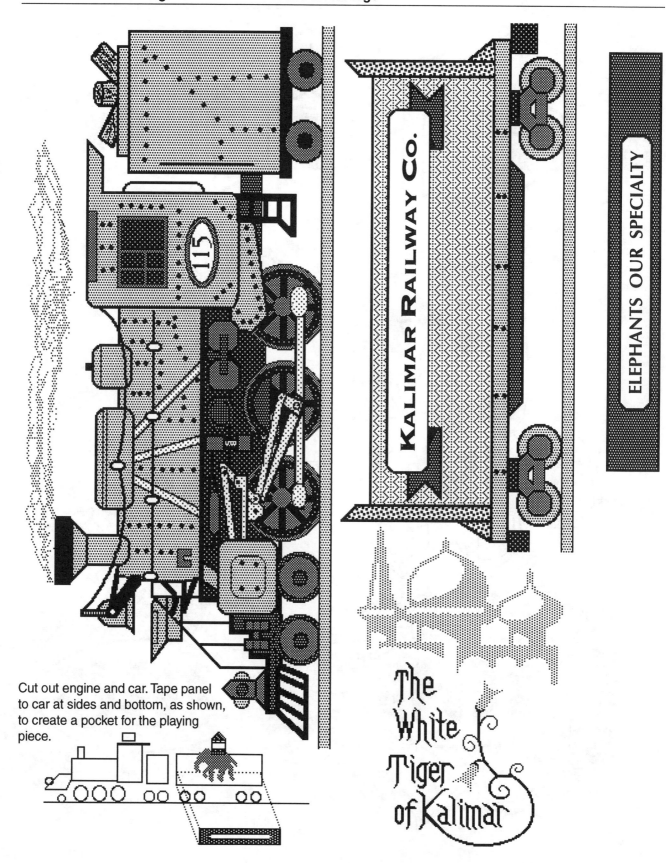

Cut out engine and car. Tape panel to car at sides and bottom, as shown, to create a pocket for the playing piece.

Kalimar Railway Co.

ELEPHANTS OUR SPECIALTY

The White Tiger of Kalimar

The Case of the Baker Street Baker

THE GAME   This is one of the more difficult games to set up because the game board requires so much detail. You may want to try simpler games before attempting this one. This Sherlock Holmes pastiche takes place in nineteenth-century London. A gang of mischievous pigs has been stealing cookies from the little bake shop on Baker Street. The baker and two of his friends set out to capture the pigs and retrieve the stolen cookies.

THE BOARD   The game board represents the streets of London. You can create this in several ways. You might choose to do a straight overhead map, something like the game board in "221B Baker Street" or other Sherlock Holmes board games. Or you might want to attempt a full-face view of several blocks of houses. If you have the talent and the time, you might want to attempt a full perspective view of several square blocks. Our artist did groupings of Victorian-era buildings in random clusters, the game path running over and around them. Your library should contain many resources for the look of nineteenth-century London buildings.

Set up a jail (or "Pig Pokey") close to the game board. This is nothing more than a cardboard box with a window cut into the front with bars to represent a jail cell. Captured pigs are placed in jail as the game progresses. (Once again, you will have to cheat now and then and remove some of the pigs after hours to prevent overcrowding of the jail.)

The game path consists of the streets of the city. Some of the spaces on the game path are covered with manhole covers. You should determine how many covers to use according to how many children are likely to play the game. The more manhole covers, the more hidden pigs and prizes you will need. The manhole covers should be

GAME 7 The Case of the Baker Street Baker: Game board

When a player lands on a manhole cover, he or she raises the cover to reveal a note telling which nearby doorway a pig is hiding behind. The door is opened and the pig is "captured" and placed in the Pig Pokey. A cookie token is then placed on the scorecard for that player.

A number of doorways on the board should be made from cardboard with tape hinges so that they can be opened to reveal a hiding pig.

Manhole covers scattered along the game path may be lifted to reveal a note describing which nearby doorway conceals a pig.

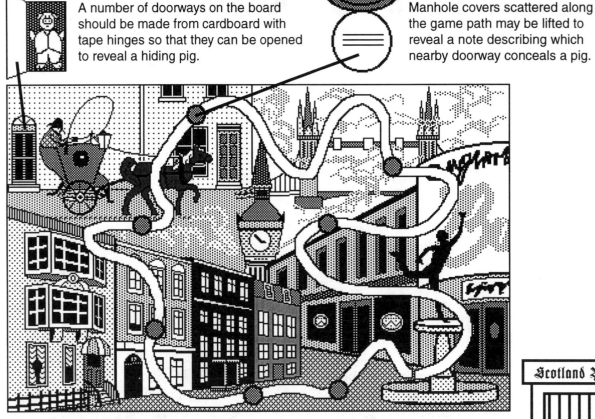

The pig pokey is just a cardboard box with a barred window on the front. Captured pigs are placed in the pokey as they are removed from the board. (Of course, new pigs must be placed behind the doors when no one is looking. You may also need to remove some of the pigs from the jail from time to time to prevent overcrowding.)

taped to the board so that they can be raised to see what is written in the square underneath. The square contains a message revealing the whereabouts of one of the pigs. This is usually in a nearby building. If you have created a street scene, provide some of the doorways with "real" paper doors that can be opened. Hide pigs behind these doors, ready to be discovered. If you have created an overhead or map-like board, you can arrange to have roofs that lift off.

When a player opens the door and captures the pig, the pig is placed in the jail. Then a cookie score token is placed on that team's scorecard. Obviously, the team with the most cookies at the end of the summer wins.

THE CHARACTERS

Our three characters this time are all animals. There are A. Conan Dog, the baker of Baker Street; Agatha Kitty, reporter for the *Times;* and Constable Gander of the Yard.

The villains in the piece are the notorious Bacon gang, consisting of a great number of pigs. We printed the pigs on pink paper before cutting them out.

SIDE TABLES

Side tables are optional with this game.

FINISHING TOUCHES

There are plenty of opportunities for decorating the children's department in keeping with the theme of the game. You might even want to set up A. Conan Dog's desk as a side table (although no side tables are required for this game). Prop the desk with a calabash pipe, deerstalker hat, magnifying glass, and a few test tubes. A few detective books would also look good there—and maybe a cookbook or two; he is a baker, after all!

GAME 7   The Case of the Baker Street Baker: Some pig villains and brochure cover

Someone is stealing cookies from the little bake shop on Baker Street. Sherlock Holmes is out of town, so the baker and his friends will try to solve the case themselves. Visit the foggy streets of London this summer, and help solve…

Ye Olde Bake Shoppe

CLOSED

The Case of the Baker Street Baker

GAME 7 The Case of the Baker Street Baker: Characters

A. Conan Dog

Agatha Kitty

Constable Gander of the Yard

GAME 7 **The Case of the Baker Street Baker: Cookie score tokens (100) and Honor Roll certificate**

GAME 7   The Case of the Baker Street Baker: Pigs

GAME 7   The Case of the Baker Street Baker: Manhole covers

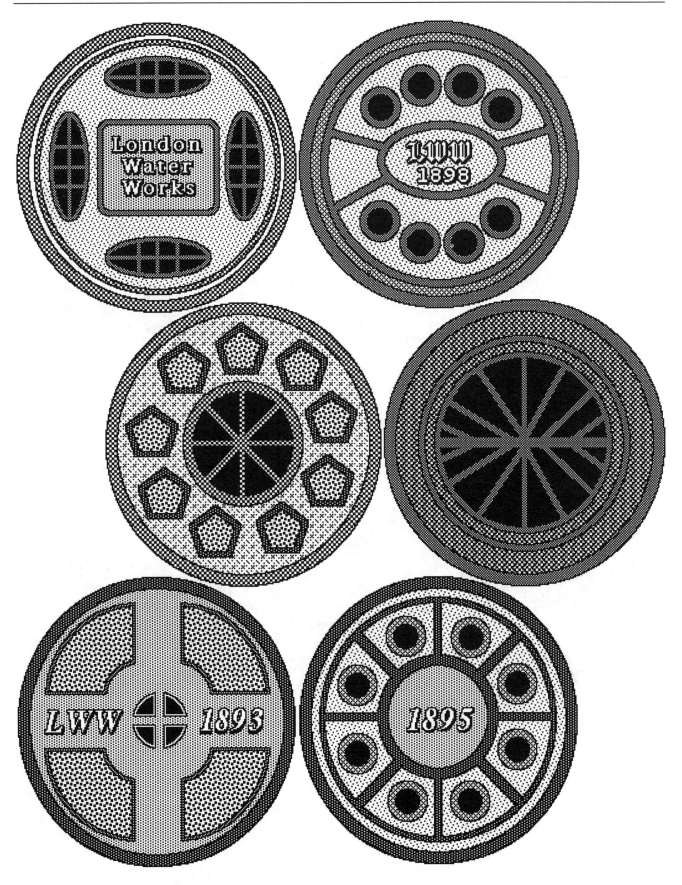

GAME 7   The Case of the Baker Street Baker: Cookie score tokens (1)

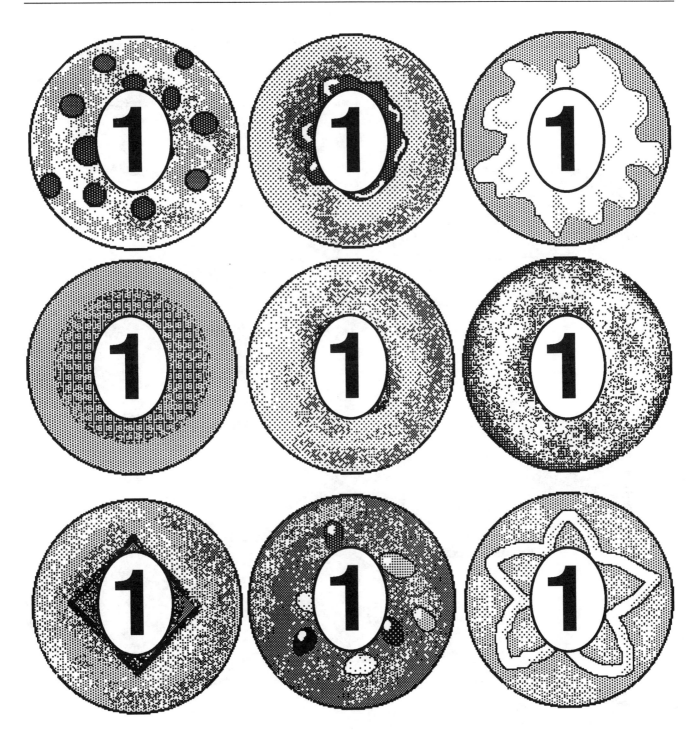

GAME 7   The Case of the Baker Street Baker: Cookie score tokens (10)

GAME 7   The Case of the Baker Street Baker: Score tokens (1000), logo, and miscellaneous art

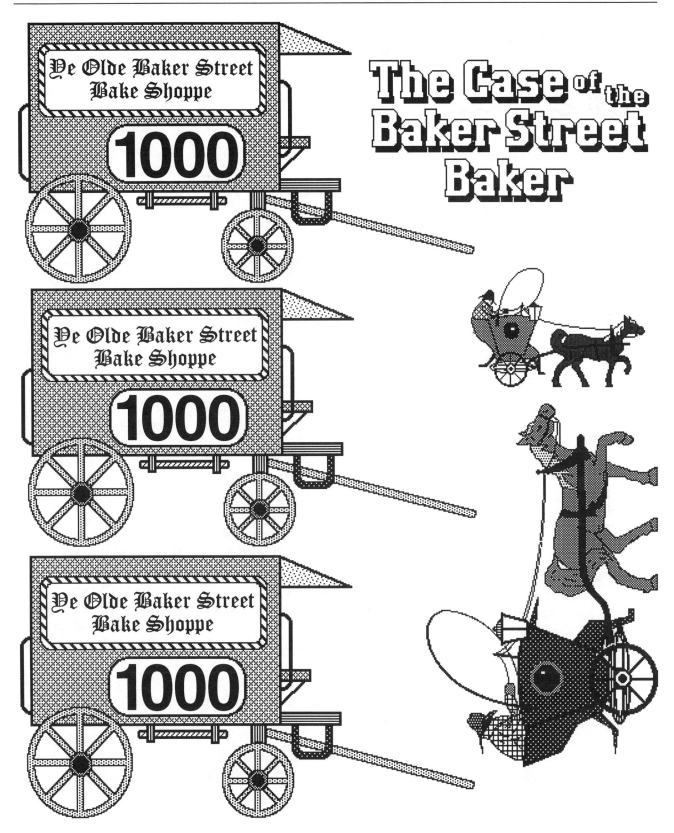

GAME **8**

●●

Highway to the Stars

THE GAME   This space adventure game involves three teams of Space Rangers preparing to capture space pirates known as the Farn. Because the requirements for the game board are fairly simple, this is one of the easiest games to set up.

THE BOARD   The board itself represents outer space, and so may be constructed using a large sheet of black or dark blue paper. Stars may be added with paint (this is a great opportunity to use up those old bottles of white-out fluid). Pastel chalks may be used to add colored stars, but be sure to spray them with fixative. Larger stars, planets, and moons may be cut from colored paper or from old astronomy posters or magazine illustrations. For a three-dimensional effect, try cutting various-size Styrofoam balls in half and painting them.

There should be two or three primary planets. It's a good idea to create some sort of creatures to inhabit these planets and to paint them or place paper cutouts of them on their respective worlds. We had one world inhabited by plant people—stick figures with green stem bodies, leaves for feet and hands, and flower blossoms for heads. You might want to consider insects or reptiles for the other planets. Finally, the home planet of the Farn should be located near one corner of the board.

Place the Space Ranger space station in the corner farthest away from the Farn planet. The station may be a disk, sphere, box, tube, or a combination of any of those. The station should be encrusted with lots of portholes, antennas poking out all over the place, radar dishes, and hatches. For a three-dimensional effect, start out with a cardboard box or tube, cover with aluminum foil, and add colored wire, bits of hardware, and colored tape. Look for the plastic containers that tiny toys from vending machines come in—they make great observation domes.

The board represents outer space with several planets, stars, and galaxies. Starting with black paper for the background, other elements can be created with such things as colored paper, paint, and aluminum foil. The game begins at the Space Ranger space station and proceeds to the home planet of the Farn. Players travel to the Farn planet, arrest a Farn, then return to the space station.

Beware of being drawn into the gravitational field of a large planet and delayed.

Worm hole. Land here and be transported to another part of the board.

Meteor cluster . . . beware of collisions!

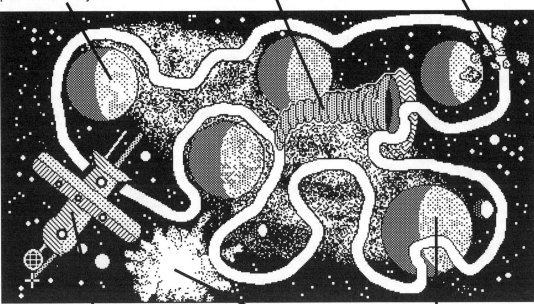

Space Rangers headquarters. Game begins and ends here.

Star exploding in a supernova.

Home planet of the Farn. Land and arrest one pirate.

The game path should meander around the board and among the planets until it finally arrives at the Farn world.

Cut out a large number of Farn spaceships and attach them to the board so that they can easily be removed. As each character arrives at the Farn planet, a Farn ship is removed and placed on that team's scorecard. We have included score tokens for 1, 10, and 100 Farns.

Keep replacing Farn ships on the board (preferably when the kids aren't watching) until the game ends, at which time the board should be free of the troublesome pests.

THE CHARACTERS

The characters consist of three members of the Space Rangers in their spaceships. One is a human girl, the others are rather cuddly aliens. We'll leave it to you to make up names for them.

SIDE TABLES

As there are no side tables for this game, specially marked squares on the game board should award prizes directly.

FINISHING TOUCHES

The Farn look like haystacks with teeth. If you wish to create a "live" version of one to put on display, you can make one by gluing straw or yarn to a large can (an old paint can would be ideal). A rounded dome-like top, also covered with straw or yarn, may be made from Styrofoam, from an inflatable ball stuffed into the top of the can, or even from a ball of crumpled newspaper. Once the proper shaggy look has been achieved, Ping-Pong ball eyes can be glued on, along with a jagged set of teeth cut from white construction paper. The Farn are usually armed with a spear, made from a wooden dowel with a cardboard point.

GAME 8   Highway to the Stars: Character no. 2 and brochure cover

Nasty haystack creatures known as the Farn are attacking the ships of other space travellers on the new interstellar highway. Three teams of Space Rangers have set out to stop the Farns once and for all. Join ▲ the excitement at the library this summer and help patrol the…

GAME 8   Highway to the Stars: Character no. 3 and Honor Roll certificate

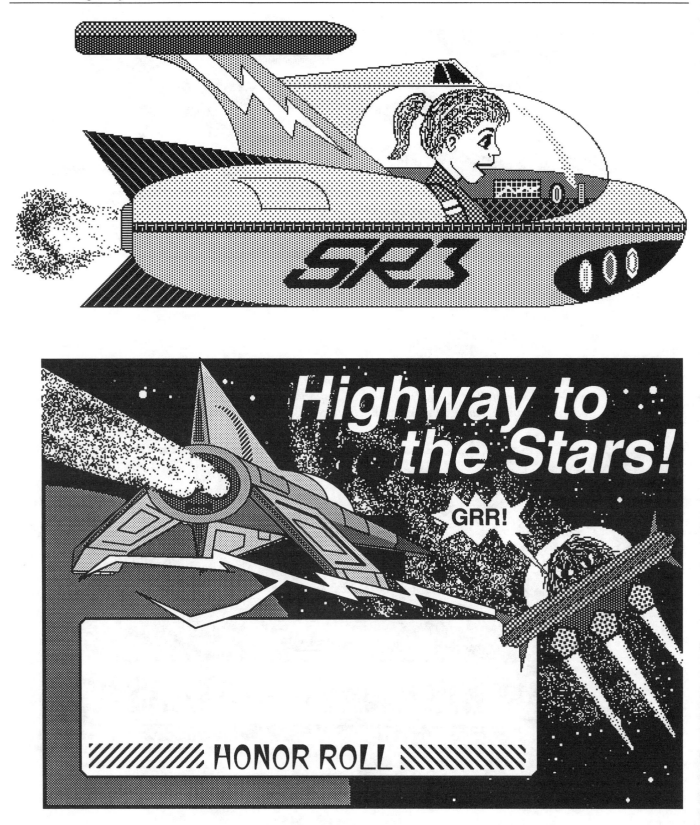

GAME 8   Highway to the Stars: Farn spaceships/score tokens (1)

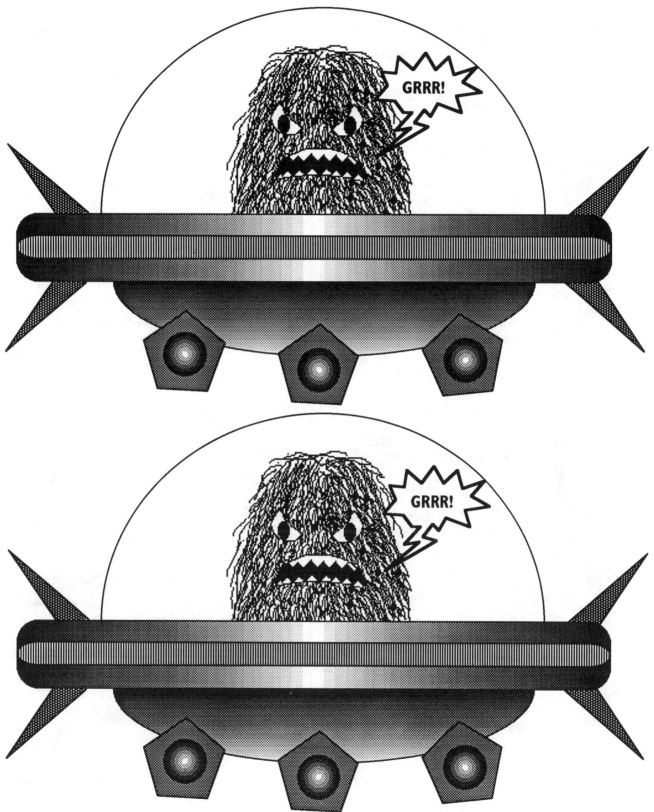

GAME 8   Highway to the Stars: Score tokens (10)

GAME 8   Highway to the Stars: Score tokens (100)

GAME 9

Lost in Time

THE GAME This is a time travel/dinosaur theme game. It is one of the simpler ones, with few extra graphics or facilities required. The premise is that two children and their dog have taken their time machine back to the age of the dinosaurs. But their time machine has run out of energy crystals, and so the three must gather enough crystals to power their ship back, or risk being lost in the past forever.

THE BOARD The game board should be a prehistoric landscape, full of mountains, jungles, volcanoes, and waterfalls. The important thing here is to include lots of dinosaurs. Make them as authentic looking as possible; today's kids know their dinos!

The time machine can be any futuristic-looking device. A transparent plastic container such as a box or globe is ideal. Decorate it with lots of electronic parts like wires, transistors, lights, and so on. The crystal cave can be created with black paper as a background. Glitter or sequins can add sparkle. Attach a container full of plastic jewels to represent the crystals.

The game path starts at the time machine in one corner of the board and ends at the cave of energy crystals at the far end of the board. Typical message squares say something like: "You are delayed by a triceratops crossing your path—choose a bookmark while you are waiting."

The scorecard tokens represent energy crystals. When a character arrives at the crystal cave, a crystal is placed on the scorecard for that team. There are denominations for 1, 10, and 100 crystals.

GAME 9   Lost in Time: Game board

The board should consist of the wildest possible prehistoric landscape, complete with waterfalls, cliffs, jagged mountains, and volcanoes. Provide lots of jungle, earthquake cracks, smoke, and fog.

Populate with dinosaurs of every description (but try to make them authentic—kids know their dinosaurs!).

Waterfall and serpent-filled lake

Dense jungle   Volcano

Time machine can be any weird looking contraption...like a flying saucer, gadget-covered box, etc.

Underground cavern

Earthquake zone

Cave of energy crystals

THE CHARACTERS   We named the characters Tina, Buzz, and Lady. We used our dog as the model for Lady (she also served as the model for the Baker of Baker Street). Of course the names are entirely optional.

SIDE TABLES   There are no side tables with this game.

GAME 9 Lost in Time: Lady (alternate view) and brochure cover

Tina, Buzz, and their dog Lady have travelled back to the age of the dinosaurs in their time machine. But the machine has run out of fuel, and unless the three friends can find the energy crystals they need for power, they may be trapped in the past forever. Join the excitement at the library this summer and help save the friends who are…

GAME 9   Lost in Time: Characters

Buzz

Tina

Lady

Tina too

GAME 9   Lost in Time: Honor Roll certificate

GAME 9   Lost in Time: Crystal score tokens (1)

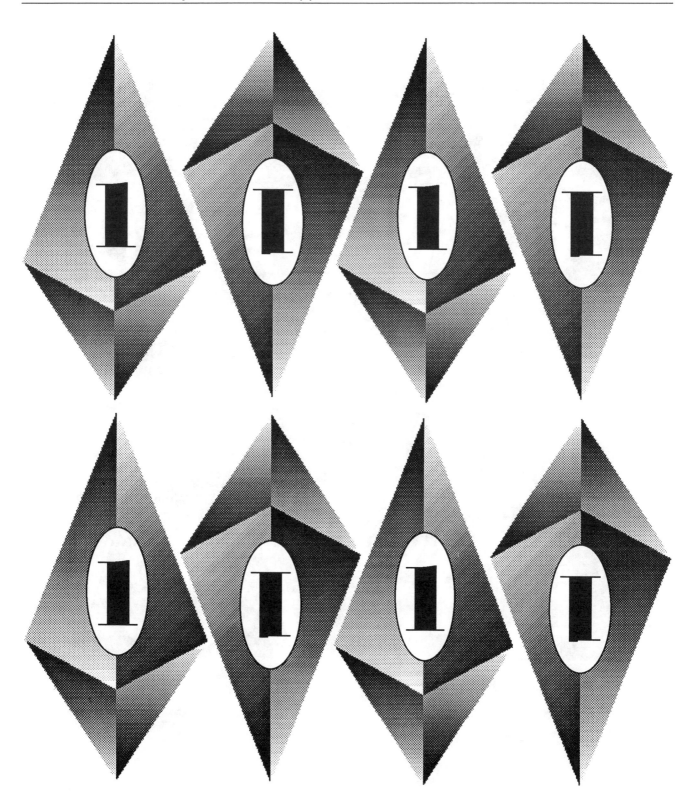

GAME 9 Lost in Time: Score tokens (10)

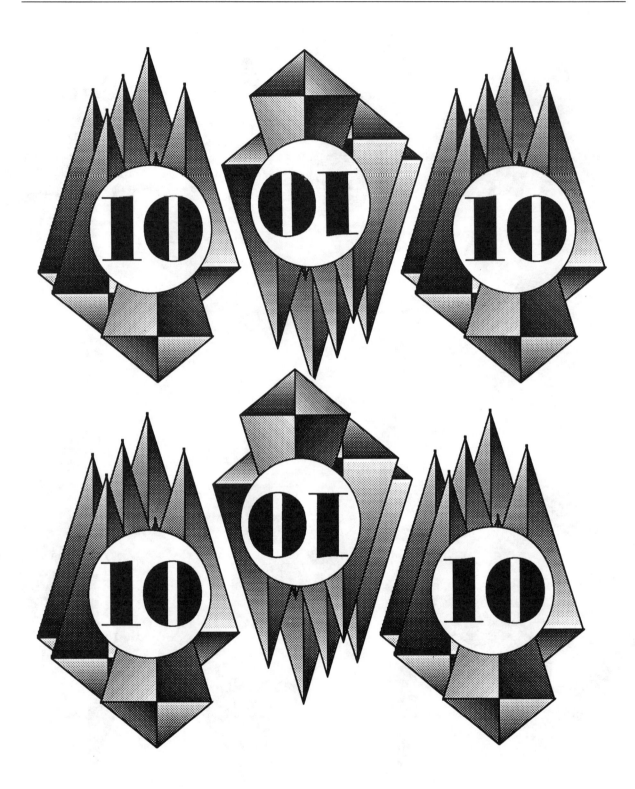

GAME 9 Lost in Time: Score tokens (100)

GAME 10

....

The Lost Library of Atlantis

THE GAME   This undersea adventure uses a lot of nautical props. A sea serpent has seized a ship full of books bound for the new library on Atlantis. The three teams will, of course, attempt to retrieve the books and restore them to the library.

THE BOARD   The game board consists of an undersea landscape, with King Neptune's palace at one end and the sea serpent's lair at the other. You may represent Atlantis by an island visible above the surface at the top of the board. Blue construction paper is a good background for the board. Coral heads and branches, giant clamshells, seaweed, and various other features may be created using colored paper—or they may be painted on. A layer of yellow sand along the bottom is fine too. Plastic plants may be attached here and there to represent seaweed.

    The sea serpent's lair should be a cave, with a built-in pocket to hold the book score tokens. A short distance before the sea serpent's lair on the game path is an oyster bed. Decorate this with pictures of seashells. Players landing on the oyster bed or its adjoining squares are directed to the oyster bed side table to obtain a pearl and a prize. The pearl may be a plastic imitation, or a cutout of silver paper. The pearl should then be attached to the playing piece with Velcro—or you may attach a small cloth "net" to the playing piece to hold the pearl. When the player arrives at the serpent's lair, the pearl is removed from the game piece and "given" to the serpent. (The pearl is later returned to the oyster bed.) A book is then taken from the lair and placed on the scorecard for that player's team.

    The team that has the most books on its scorecard at the end of the summer wins.

GAME 10   The Lost Library of Atlantis: Game board and score tokens (10)

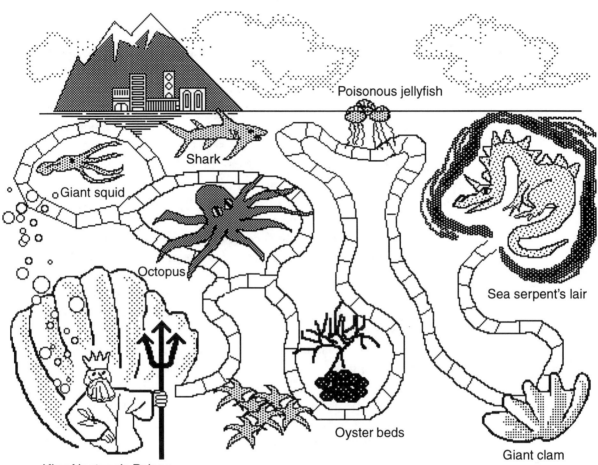

Poisonous jellyfish

Shark

Giant squid

Octopus

Sea serpent's lair

Oyster beds

Giant clam

King Neptune's Palace

The game begins at King Neptune's Palace and ends at the sea serpent's lair, where a book score token is then placed on the player's scorecard. The player returns to the Palace to start again.

THE CHARACTERS   The characters are a diver, a mermaid, and a seahorse. We called them Diver Dan, Mermaid Molly, and the Seahorse Prince, but you can give them any names you choose.

SIDE TABLES   There may be up to three side tables with this game, although one may be sufficient in smaller areas. If only one table is used, it should be the oyster bed. Construct a dry "undersea" landscape of rocks, sand, starfish, and coral. Plastic plants may be used for seaweed. Pile a number of oyster shells in the bed, with numbers painted on the underside. When directed to this side table from the game board, the player turns a shell over to reveal the number that determines the prize. Pet shops can usually supply all the plastic coral, rocks, seashells, and plants you need. If you want to use real oyster shells, a local seafood restaurant may be able to supply them.

The aquarium on the second side table can be filled with real water, and decorated with props from a pet supply shop. Small magnets or steel tokens with numbers painted on them are dropped to the bottom, and a "fishing pole" with a magnet on the end of a string is used by the players to fish out one of the numbers. Teacher supply stores may be able to provide plastic-coated magnets that will not rust in the water. Otherwise you may have to remove the magnets each evening before closing. You may, of course, create a dry version of this table using the same aquarium, but without water. (Note: This should not be a contest. Getting a number should be as easy as possible. Every child referred to any side table should get a prize.)

The third side table is an undersea pirate's treasure chest. Prop this table accordingly with such things as fishing nets, seashells, fishing floats, rocks, coral, seaweed, and a Jolly Roger flag. A crudely-scrawled sign that says "BEWARE" and a plastic skull can add a shivery touch. The centerpiece of the table is a treasure chest. This can be an old trunk, jewelry case, or even a box. Just make it look old and creepy. Inside you may use gold chocolate coins or costume jewelry with numbers painted on them. Once again, many of these props may be obtained from a pet shop or borrowed from people you know.

GAME 10   The Lost Library of Atlantis: Score tokens (100) and brochure cover

The Lost Library of Atlantis

A shipload of books, bound for the new library at Atlantis, has been captured by a sea serpent. Three brave teams will try to sneak into the serpent's lair and bring the books back.

Join the fun at the library this summer, and help rescue…

GAME 10   The Lost Library of Atlantis: Characters

Diver Dan

Mermaid Molly

Seahorse Prince

GAME 10   The Lost Library of Atlantis: Score tokens (100) and Honor Roll certificate

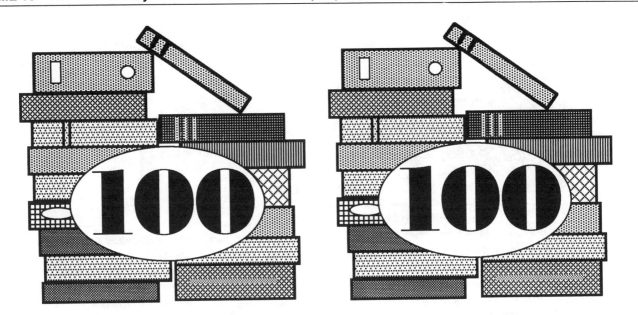

GAME 10   The Lost Library of Atlantis: Side tables and score tokens (10)

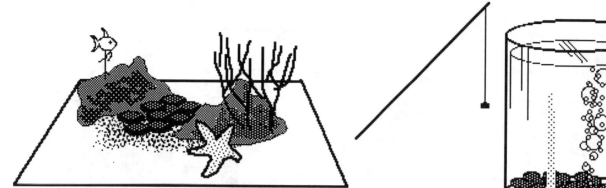

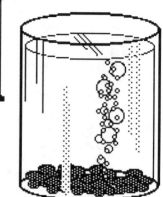

"Oyster bed" side table propped with sand, rocks, coral, starfish. Plastic versions of these may be obtained at an aquarium supply store or pet shop.

Seashells with numbers taped to the underside may be used to allow the player to select a prize.

A real aquarium filled with water and propped with seashells and other decorations obtained from a pet shop. A "fishing pole" consisting of a stick with a string with a small magnet attached is used to fish steel prize tokens from the bottom. (Tokens will have to be removed daily and dried to prevent rust from accumulating.)

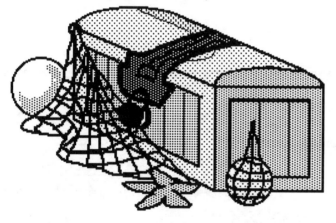

Another possibility is a sea chest (small versions designed as humidors or jewelry cases are best) propped with nets, fishing floats, seashells, etc. Inside, chocolate gold coins or costume jewelry with numbers taped to them serve as prize selection devices.

GAME 10   The Lost Library of Atlantis: Score tokens (1)

Scheduling Your Program

A TYPICAL SCHEDULE With so many details to consider, it is important to schedule your summer reading program carefully. What follows is a suggested schedule for a typical program. Obviously you will want to adapt the schedule based on available staffing, the size of your library, and the population served.

January–February Initial planning for the summer reading program begins. (If you are using one of the games in this book, most of the material in this section has already been taken care of.) Choose a subject and identify the resources needed for your program. Such resources may include artwork, construction materials, staff availability, space, and volunteers. Next write a proposal that includes a statement of the theme, a sketch of the game board, suggestions regarding characters/teams, how points will be tallied on the scorecards, suggestions for the side tables, and ideas on sources for the materials required. Present this first proposal to your staff and solicit suggestions. Finally write up your finished proposal and submit it to the staff for final approval.

March–April Contact local businesses to arrange for prizes. Be sure the terms of each prize offer or coupon offer are clearly understood by both parties. Have the program brochures and prize coupons printed, and create posters to advertise the program. Begin constructing the game board. Gather the props and decorations required for the side tables.

May School visits begin. Members of the library staff should visit each kindergarten through fifth-grade classroom in your service area. Bring your posters to classrooms and distribute your brochures.

Describe the program to the children, and emphasize the prizes and fun. Submit press releases about the program to local newspapers—be sure to include graphics, such as your logo. Finish the game board and prepare it for installation. Make sure you have all necessary props, small prizes, and decorations for the side tables. Send ads soliciting STAR volunteers to the local junior high and high schools.

June   Install the game board and set up the side tables. Train your STAR volunteers. Finalize the volunteers' schedules no more than seven to ten days before they start work, since kids tend to forget appointments beyond that. The program should start some time in June, shortly after school lets out.

August   At our library, the game lasts eight weeks, usually ending after the first full week in August. After the game is over, the Honor Roll certificates are made out, then mailed to the schools in time for distribution during the first week of classes.

Designing Your Own Game

After looking at some of the games in this book, you may wish to design your own. This is especially desirable if there is some local event or festival that you would like to capitalize on in your game. For example, you might want to design a game relating to the anniversary of the founding of your town.

Although designing your own game will obviously require extra effort, you may find it worthwhile if you and your staff have the time and the abilities. Here are a few tips to help you put your own game together.

**CHOOSING
A THEME**

Choose a theme that appeals to your target age group. (If it is an election year, remember that political themes must make sense to young children.) Movies that receive a great deal of publicity in your area can also suggest themes. Every now and then, for example, dinosaurs or space aliens make a big splash in the movies. Games involving those elements are obviously a good idea at such times. Of course, you will want to avoid possible copyright problems, so don't follow the movie theme too closely.

Avoid didactic subjects. Children have a sixth sense that tells them when we are trying to slip academic information to them under the guise of fun. Kids are glad to be out of school for the summer, and we don't believe it is a good idea to make them feel that by going to the library they are returning to the classroom. Children already see the library as a learning resource; the summer program can encourage them to turn to the library for enjoyment as well. Ideally we want the children to benefit from the content of the books. The game is just to challenge them to keep reading.

In choosing your theme, keep in mind the basic structure of the board game itself. Ask yourself these questions: What is the point of the game? (Capturing villains; paying a ransom; accumulating objects.)

How may this best be translated into accumulating points? (Number of villains in jail; number of jewels paid in ransom; golden bricks retrieved from a cave.) And what is the best way to represent them graphically on the scorecard? (Pictures of captured villains; paper cutout diamonds; gold paper bricks.)

Your theme will usually generate ideas for suitable characters. Depending on the subject, you might wish to make them explorers, scientists, astronauts, knights, or animals or other whimsical creatures. For more exotic themes you can let your imagination run wild. We once created a race of space aliens that were plants, with stems and leaves for limbs and flowers for faces.

The art and lettering used in your program should suit your theme. A wild west theme, for example, would suggest lots of woodgrain, Barnum-style lettering, cattle brands, etc. You may find, as we have, that your game develops around one or two ideas simply because they are available. "The White Tiger of Kalimar" was inspired by a digitized photograph of a tiger that happened to be included with our new computer. In another example, a visit to the library by a speaker from the Shedd Aquarium suggested the underwater theme that was developed into "The Lost Library of Atlantis."

DEVELOPING THE GRAPHICS

Once your core idea has been chosen, artwork for the various materials necessary must be located. Magazines, travel agencies, historical societies, and your own library's collection are great places to start.

Clip Art

Some of the artwork selected for your program should be used to produce your personal collection of clip art. Look for simple images that convey the idea of the game. Commercial clip art is usually published in books or on computer disks according to theme, i.e., holidays, business, travel, and animals. You may have used clip art in newsletters, school materials, and the like. If you do not have access to commercial clip art, here's how to make some of your own.

You will need good black and white artwork related to your theme. Most of this artwork should be line art, that is, it should be composed of solid blacks and whites with no continuous gray tones. This type of art reproduces easily on photocopiers, and is usually the least expensive to have printed by commercial printers. Use your computer if it can produce black and white art and print it out. Almost any software designed to make greeting cards, newsletters, or banners will work. Print shops can often scan art onto a computer disk for you, converting it to black and white in the process.

If you do not have access to a computer, you may convert gray-toned or colored artwork to black and white in various ways. Line art can usually be converted simply by copying it with your photocopier on the high-contrast setting. Or you might try tracing it on thin paper with black ink.

Once you have a collection of black and white line art related to your theme, paste the artwork onto 8½-by-11-inch paper. Then make high-quality copies of these sheets and your clip art is ready to be cut out and pasted down in different arrangements on your various materials.

The Logo   It is a good idea to create some sort of logo for your program. This is usually a simple graphic or lettering highlighting the name of your program. The logo for "The White Tiger of Kalimar" was created on our computer by modifying stock letters and creating the Indian-style buildings in a graphics program. A similar design could readily be created with pen and ink, of course. In order to avoid scaling difficulties, the logo should be created in the size most often used. Notice that our logos are reproduced in the same size on brochures, honor roll certificates, coupons, etc. Some copy machines or local graphic art companies can provide enlarged or reduced copies of your logo if needed. Your logo is important because it will serve to identify your program to the community. The brochures, buttons, and coupons on which it appears will be distributed throughout the area. Honor Roll certificates with the logo will be found on bedroom walls and stuck to refrigerators with little magnets for years to come, serving as constant reminders of your library's quality service. Don't forget to include the logo on any press releases you issue to local papers.

PROMOTIONAL MATERIAL   Once your logo has been developed, it should be incorporated into as many of the materials used in your program as possible. Here is a list of the materials used in a typical program.

Brochures   These are handed out to classes during school visiting and to all children who visit the library in the weeks prior to the start of the program. The brochure is your primary form of advertising, and so should be as exciting as possible. Devote as much space as possible to artwork connected with the game theme. This is also another place for your logo. A small amount of text should explain the theme of the game, and include the name of your library and the dates of the game. See chapter 3 for instructions on preparing your brochure for printing.

Honor Roll Certificates   Your certificate should contain artwork from the brochure, the logo, and possibly a fancy gold sticker. The child's name is typed on the certificate, which is then signed by the children's librarian. See chapter 3 for suggestions on having the certificates printed.

Coupons   Some libraries use coupons that have been produced by local fast-food restaurants. That is fine. However, don't overlook potential sponsors in your community who would perhaps be delighted to help sponsor your program if you would offer to develop and print coupons for them. We do that very successfully with several local restaurants (see page 10).

All the elements of your game need to be carefully scheduled in order to have them ready as summer starts. See appendix A for suggestions on how to schedule your program.

Suggestions for Game Board Construction

Most of our boards were produced in the library by an artist on the staff. If you do not have such a person on your staff, check other sources in the community. Contact local schools to see who teaches art, or contact local crafts organizations. Often, all it takes is a request to locate talented volunteers who would love to help the children in this way.

If you cannot find an artist in your community, it is still possible to create an interesting game board on your own.

There are two basic approaches to creating a board. One consists in creating a single large picture that includes all the scenic elements as if they were part of one scene. The landscapes for such games as "The White Tiger of Kalimar" or "The Lost City of the Aztecs" are examples of this type of approach. In general it is best to avoid a direct overhead perspective. For one thing, it is often difficult to tell what an object is when viewed from above. And while this might work in the floor plan of a house, as in "The Haunted Mansion," it is not so effective in representing natural areas, or larger areas such as the city of London in "Baker Street Baker." For these reasons, it is best to illustrate scenic areas from an angle, as if viewed from a cliff or tall building. This may be a fairly challenging type of board, since all the various elements should fit together proportionally and in scale to make a believable landscape.

Another approach is the "zone" approach, in which the board is divided up into a series of smaller sections, each depicting a part of the overall theme. For example, rather than create a detailed cross section of a house as shown in the game board sketch for "The Monster Bash," our artist divided the game board into different-sized rectangles, each representing a room in the house. Each room could thus be decorated and filled with goofy monsters separately, without worrying if it matched in proportion or perspective to the entire board. In one room she pasted a cutout of a famous picture of card-playing dogs; in another she combined photographs of a grotesque table with a picture of a checkerboard and small pictures of various monsters as pieces. (See Figure A.1.)

Once the approach is chosen, it's time to create a background. A background may be made easily from colored construction paper. Photographic supply stores sell large rolls of seamless background paper which is ideal for this purpose.

Once your background has been established, artwork from various sources may be pasted, copied, or painted onto it. Possible sources for such artwork include magazines, calendars, art prints, travel agencies, posters, and so on. For "The White Tiger of Kalimar," our artist assembled pictures on India from *National Geographic* and other discarded magazines. These were used as models for painting on the board. We also obtained travel posters and brochures on India from local travel agencies. These sources provided excellent examples of Indian landscape, architecture, dress, and animal life.

Three-dimensional forms can be added to your game board using Styrofoam boulders or glaciers, sandpaper deserts, knitting-yarn spider webs, and clear plastic-sheet lakes. Hobby stores and novelty shops can provide an endless variety of trees, building fronts, plastic spaceships, boats, dinosaurs, spiders, snakes, and aliens. Suggestions for specific items are included with games in this book. Figure A.2 shows some general tips which may be used in any game.

Check the size of your playing pieces to be sure the various elements on the board are not too large or too small in relation to the characters. Here again, the zone system lets you work in much smaller areas, making it convenient for working on a desktop.

FIGURE A.1   Two approaches to constructing the game board

Game board for the "Monster Bash" as shown on page 48. This represents a single scene, and some people may find it difficult to create.

Game board for "Monster Bash" in which the board is divided up into individual small scenes. Each scene may be constructed separately, providing an easier design and construction challenge.

FIGURE A.2   Scenery suggestions

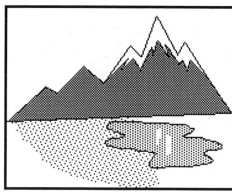

Most scenery elements can be put together from colored paper. Rocks, shadows, and other details can be painted on or cut from contrasting colored paper.

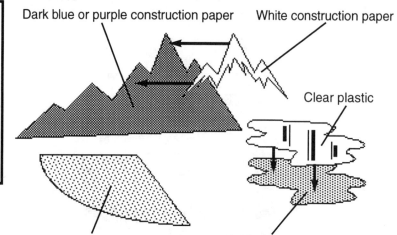

Dark blue or purple construction paper   White construction paper

Clear plastic

Tan construction paper or sandpaper   Light blue construction paper

Castles and other buildings can be created from colored construction paper. To add a 3-dimensional effect, make towers from paper tubes and cones cut in half.

Trees can be made from black or brown construction paper or from twigs. Glue chopped green yarn to the branches for leaves.

Rustic gates and doors can be made from wooden tongue depressors or Popsicle sticks.

Black paper or steel wool smoke

Yellow or orange paper flames

Red and orange paper for lava ... or better yet, red or orange foil

Dark brown or charcoal gray paper mountain

Wayne Johnson has designed the summer reading programs at the Glenview (Illinois) Public Library for the past fifteen years. His published work includes photographs, magazine articles, movie and book reviews—as well as the first critical study of the science fiction writer Ray Bradbury. Wayne's background includes coconut rehabilitation in the Western Pacific as a Peace Corps volunteer and advertising copywriting for large commercial catalogs; he is a native of Oak Park, Illinois.

Yvette Johnson has been head of Youth Services at the Glenview (Illinois) Public Library for twenty years. She has contributed articles to *Journal of Youth Services* and *Illinois Libraries* as well as a chapter in the ALA Editions book *Youth Services Librarians as Managers*. She has served on the Board of the Illinois Library Association and was head of the task force that revised standards for youth services in Illinois public libraries (1993). She received her MSLS degree from Dominican University (Rosary College) in 1978.